Future-proofed

Ilia Antenucci

Future-proofed

The Speculative Life of Smart Cities

Ilia Antenucci
Gran Sasso Science Institute
L'Aquila, Italy

ISBN 978-3-031-86428-5   ISBN 978-3-031-86429-2   (eBook)
https://doi.org/10.1007/978-3-031-86429-2

The development of this book was supported by the project 'Automating the Logistical City', funded by Lower Saxony DIGITAL CREATIVITY175 Ministry of Science and Culture and the Niedersächsisches Vorab's call for proposals on 'DigitalSociety' (Grant ID ZN 3752).

© The Editor(s) (if applicable) and The Author(s), under exclusive license to Springer Nature Switzerland AG 2025

This work is subject to copyright. All rights are solely and exclusively licensed by the Publisher, whether the whole or part of the material is concerned, specifically the rights of translation, reprinting, reuse of illustrations, recitation, broadcasting, reproduction on microfilms or in any other physical way, and transmission or information storage and retrieval, electronic adaptation, computer software, or by similar or dissimilar methodology now known or hereafter developed.
The use of general descriptive names, registered names, trademarks, service marks, etc. in this publication does not imply, even in the absence of a specific statement, that such names are exempt from the relevant protective laws and regulations and therefore free for general use.
The publisher, the authors and the editors are safe to assume that the advice and information in this book are believed to be true and accurate at the date of publication. Neither the publisher nor the authors or the editors give a warranty, expressed or implied, with respect to the material contained herein or for any errors or omissions that may have been made. The publisher remains neutral with regard to jurisdictional claims in published maps and institutional affiliations.

This Palgrave Macmillan imprint is published by the registered company Springer Nature Switzerland AG
The registered company address is: Gewerbestrasse 11, 6330 Cham, Switzerland

If disposing of this product, please recycle the paper.

A Very Brief Preface

When I started the doctoral research project on which this book is based, 'smart' was the word of the moment—self-evidently good, uncritically embraced, and ubiquitous. Fast forward a few years, and smart cities no longer inspire TED Talks at quite the same rate. A bit like yesterday's blockchain, smart cities are still around, still influential, but no longer the shiny object that everyone is scrambling to name-drop first chance they get. Some high-profile projects collapsed under their own weight, while others simply fizzled out, revealing the ever-expanding gap between promise and reality. Digital governance isn't as seamless as promised, predictive algorithms get things wrong all the time, and the much-hyped urban AI revolution is still mostly trying to figure out how to synchronise traffic lights without causing gridlock. And yet, while the *term* might be fading from the spotlight, the *logics* and the *forces* of smart urbanism—data-driven governance, platform capitalism, and the algorithmic optimisation of everyday life—continue to shape our cities in ways that demand attention. This book is not a post-mortem on the smart city, but an exploration of its speculative life: the ways in which digital technologies, financial operations, and urban governance collide to produce futures that are as uncertain as they are ambitious.

As I write this preface, I may not even be the one writing it—an AI assistant might be doing a fine job in my place. The infrastructures that shape daily life—data, money, security, even the words on this page—are more entangled with speculative technologies than ever. Meanwhile, a

vi A VERY BRIEF PREFACE

few tech oligarchs have just waltzed into the White House, laying hands on decisions that will impact millions of people around the world. The same people who built the platforms that shape our cities, economies, and politics are now in a position to set the policies that govern them. At this point, understanding how speculative infrastructures hit the ground isn't just an intellectual exercise; it's a political necessity and a survival skill.

L'Aquila, Italy   Ilia Antenucci
June 10th 2025

Acknowledgements

It takes a village to write a book. It is a labour of love and persistence that I could not have done without the inputs and support from the extended village of colleagues, friends, and family that I have been lucky enough to rely on.

Andrea Pollio is the best friend I could hope for and the best scholar I know in one person. Thank you for sharing your faboulous brain with me so generously, and for the wonderful times we had over the past ten years. Armin Beverungen and Maja-Lee Voigt have been wonderful colleagues and friends. Thank you for teaching me so much, for your solidarity and your humour. Working with you for the past three years has been a privilege and a joy. I am also forever grateful to Brett Neilson and Ned Rossiter, my Ph.D. supervisors, for their gentle guidance and for providing me with tools—both theoretical and ethical—that I keep using every day. The wit and intellectual fireworks of Mithilesh Kumar are with me every day across continents and long years of distance—thank you, my friend. And a heartfelt thank goes to Ugo Rossi, who more than anyone else encouraged and motivated me to start and, more importantly, to finish this book.

Last but not least, my life is blessed with beautiful people who make every day better: thank you to Agnese, Eleonora, Eugenia, and Martina e Valeria, just for being around. To mamma, papà, and Marta, for still bearing with me after so many years. And finally, to Luigi and Nives, who are everything; and to P, my grumpy husband, the one and only.

CONTENTS

1 Introduction — 1
Smart Cities? — 4
Why Smart Cities Are Speculative — 7
The Unlikely Smart Cities — 13
Speculation as Method — 18
Outline of the Chapters — 21
References — 23

2 Speculative Urbanism: Transforming the Present Through the Future — 27
The Ghost City Goes Smart — 29
Africa's Smartest City — 36
Tech Chimeras and Urban Transformation — 41
    The Bengal Silicon Valley — 41
    The Silicon Cape — 46
Broader than Finance — 51
References — 53

3 Testbed Cities: Experiments, Prototypes, Trials — 59
Testbeds and Tests — 63
Drones — 66
Automating the City — 70
Testing (as) Urban Governance — 73
References — 81

ix

x CONTENTS

4 Futures and Failures: How Speculative Algorithms (Try to) Run the City 83
'Security Goes EPIC in Cape Town' 85
Listening to the Voice of Citizens? 90
Surveillance, Dataveillance, and Beyond 94
Security Speculations 98
Realtimeness and Preemption 106
When Algorithms Fail 108
References 111

5 From Land to Data: Money in the Smart City 117
Data, Value, Extractions (s) 118
Land Grabbing, Gentrification, and the Work of Finance 121
Platforms and Their Discontents 127
Urban Mining 133
Speculation and Extraction Beyond Surveillance 139
References 144

6 Beyond the Smart City: Speculating Otherwise 149
Futures 151
The Banality of Urban Speculations 153
Other Speculations: The Right to the AI City? 156
References 160

List of Interviews and Personal Conversations 165

Index 167

CHAPTER 1

Introduction

In 2017, following several car accidents, the last of which killed a six-year-old child, the New Town Kolkata Development Authority passed a much-awaited bylaw, ordering the seizure of stray cattle on the streets. This happened almost two years after the official announcement that this unfinished, desolate satellite township on the outskirts of Kolkata would become a smart city. In the previous decade, farmlands had been expropriated to build high-rises, and many farmers took up precarious jobs as construction workers to support their families. But at some point investors pulled out and construction slowed down or stopped completely. Left without land or jobs, the former farmers let the cattle they couldn't feed anymore roam loose. The cows, for their part, did not lose heart and found subsistence in the grass and plants that had been created for the sake of 'beautification' around the Main Arterial Road of New Town, where high-speed Wi-Fi was first installed and Bengal Silicon Valley is supposed to rise.

Not long afterwards, in Cape Town, allegedly Africa's smartest city, people were queuing up to fill water jugs from a natural spring at the foot of Table Mountain. The long-announced water crisis had hit at last, dams were at their lowest level in a century, and the menace of Day Zero—when taps would have to be shut off—was looming. Over the past decades, huge investments had been made in smart infrastructure—broadband fibre, sensors, and software—in an effort to make the city more

© The Author(s), under exclusive license to Springer Nature
Switzerland AG 2025
I. Antenucci, *Future-proofed*,
https://doi.org/10.1007/978-3-031-86429-2_1

1

efficient and sustainable. No technology, however, could avert the water crisis. In the offices of city managers, dashboards displayed real-time maps of water consumption and models of dam levels; inside the houses of Capetonians, smart meters enforced water restrictions. Those who could afford it were having boreholes dug in their gardens to reach underwater reservoirs; those who couldn't, queued for water under the sun.

These are two short glimpses of New Town Kolkata and Cape Town—two cities that were meant to become 'smart'. This book tells the stories of their making: stories of speculations on and through technologies, economies, and governance. By speculations, here, I refer to a broad range of operations, often intertwined, which seek to appropriate and shape the future. The paths to urban digitalisation of New Town and Cape Town are very different, but both marked by sharp inequalities, colonial legacies, and developmental imperatives. In both cities, smart city projects are speculative in that they might never materialise in the promised final form, yet mobilise narratives and expectations that transform urban environments in socio-economic terms. Speculations turn urban spaces into testbeds for a growing range of new technological solutions, where experiments become a new mode of governance and valorisation. But smart cities are also speculative insofar as they are increasingly governed through algorithmic technologies, which model possible futures in the attempt to make them actionable in the present. And, last but not least, smart cities are also fuelled by financial operations, from venture capital funding tech startups, to real estate initiatives, to commercial platforms which bet on, and try to shape, the future configurations of the city. Overall, speculation acts as both a logic and a force of urban transformation through digital technologies, creating new modes of knowing, governing, and monetising the city.

For about fifteen years, between the late 2010s and the Covid-19 pandemic, the smart city was a very popular concept. This label has been attached to urban processes of different kinds and scale—from the mere rolling out of public Wi-Fi in provincial towns, to the creation of brand new mega cities, such as Songdo or Masdar. As digital infrastructures and platforms began to proliferate across urban spaces, they were packaged into narratives of efficiency, smoothness, transparency, and sustainability. I challenge these all too popular tales and demonstrate how smart city projects have been built on technologies that speculate on the future to govern the present, both politically and financially, with implications for spatial justice and urban rights. These days, smart cities may sound a bit dated, but digital infrastructures are every day more powerful and pervasive across every field of life. It is thus vital to build discerning insights into the logics that inform computing technologies, into the networks of knowledge, power, and money through which they are developed, and into the societal effects they generate. This book contributes to this critical knowledge by unpacking the speculative logic of smart city projects. Drawing on case studies from New Town Kolkata and Cape Town, the book explores how speculative operations intersect postcolonial conditions, creating situated configurations of infrastructures, governance, and economies. In doing this, I join a cohort of authors who have been bringing the focus on smart and, more broadly, digital urbanism in Africa, Asia, and South America, thus contributing to dislocating theoretical production away from the still too dominant 'Global North' focus (Cirolia et al., 2023; Datta, 2015; Datta & Shaban, 2023; Edensor & Jayne, 2011; Parnell & Robinson, 2013; Pollio, 2020). Critiques of smart cities are of course not new, but most of them so far have tackled essentially two aspects: the rise of corporate power, coupled with a shift of urban governance towards technocracy (Hollands, 2015; Kitchin & Perng, 2016; Kitchin et al., 2019; Perng & Maalsen, 2020; Söderström et al., 2020; Sadowski & Bendor, 2019; Savini & Raco, 2021) and the functions of surveillance that smart urban technologies creepily perform (Galdon-Clavell, 2013; Melgaço & Van Brakel, 2021; Monahan, 2018; Wood & Mackinnon, 2019). Both lines of inquiry are key to understanding the perils for social justice and democracy, especially concerning marginalised communities, which arise when urban governance is entrusted to big data and algorithms. This book picks a different angle. If surveillance and corporate power are certainly problematic features of smart city projects, more is at stake there. As computing technologies rewire urban environments, they do more than collect data, breach privacy, or generate revenues for tech companies. They are making, or breaking, specific urban futures. Those are not neutral, but informed by power relations, political goals, and profit strategies. This is what I call the power of speculation. This runs, as Keller Easterling (2014) explains, through the technological properties of infrastructures and is, as Jennifer Gabrys (2016) makes clear, ontogenetic. By looking closely at the ways in which speculation informs urban designs, computing techniques, practices of governance, and value extraction in the making of smart cities, this book casts new light on the ways in which

4   I. ANTENUCCI

these urban experiments have transformed decision-making, rights, and economic power.

SMART CITIES?

As I write this book, smart cities have lost at least some hype. Among urban designers and policymakers, activists and journalists, scepticism seems to have grown around the idea that big data and algorithms could somehow miraculously deliver efficient infrastructures and better governance. Yet for a few years over the past decade making cities 'smarter' by fitting them with as many sensors, chips, and data management software, looked like the ultimate solution to all urban problems, and the latest frontier of urban transformation. Unsurprisingly, there was a commercial substrate to it. As Anthony Townsend (2015) notes, the idea of using large-scale computer models to address urban problems goes back to the 1960s in the US, when defence consultants like the RAND Institute tried to apply predictive models used in military planning to urban issues, with unsuccessful results. During the 1990s, urban modelling came back in the US through more limited experiments, such as the CompStat used by the New York Police Department. Then, at some point, the smart city became a full-fledged commercial product. In 2008, Sam Palmisano, then CEO of IBM, gave a public talk on the idea of building a smarter planet made up of smarter cities. At the time, the company was seeking to reposition itself in the market, from hardware to software producer (Söderström et al., 2014). Soon after Palmisano's talk, IBM registered the trademark 'smarter cities' and launched an aggressive marketing campaign to sell software for urban management. The campaign narrative described contemporary cities as 'sick' from various pathologies, such as tightening budgets, growing population, pollution, and inefficient administration. IBM promised that smart technologies could heal them all. Cities become 'smart', IBM claimed, as implicitly opposed to 'dumb', when they gather as much data as possible, run them through algorithms that generate models, and use the models to make decisions. For Söderström et al. (2014), smart city narratives present a distinct version of urban utopia where the perfect integration of computing systems would ensure complete efficiency. This 'mild utopianism', grounded in the commercial purpose of selling specific technologies, does not require 'the replacement of existing spaces, but its digital redoubling' (Söderström et al., 2014, p. 316). The model quickly gained momentum among other tech players, such as Microsoft, Cisco, Intel, Oracle, SAP, and Google—each of which launched its own set of smart city products. But the corporate sector was not alone in pursuing urban digitalisation. Since the early 2000s, universities across all continents have increasingly established research centres and programmes devoted to applying data science and computer science to urban systems. The Senseable City Lab at MIT, the Data Science Institute at the Columbia University, the Urban Analytics Lab at the National University of Singapore, the Urban Predictive Analytics Lab at the University of British Columbia are only few among the numerous examples. Well-funded and influential, these academic clusters are developing what Townsend (2015) calls a 'new urban science', concerned with designing tools for large-scale data analysis in service of policymaking. This science is shaped by the assumption that data are a medium of superior knowledge, what José Van Dijck (2014) defines as *dataism*. As Dietmar Offenhuber and Carlo Ratti (2014) from the MIT Senseable City Lab, write: 'Data allows us to model the highly dynamic nature of cities, their social life, and their infrastructure networks at an unprecedented level of detail' (2014, p. 13). Political discourses at any scale—from the United Nations to small municipalities—were quick in appropriating and mobilising the storyline of data and algorithms as synonyms of innovation, sustainability, and better urban governance. Cities around the world—from big 'global' metropolises to small, provincial towns—have eagerly embraced investments in sensing technologies and software. From Hudson Yards in New York to the (failed) project of Google Sidewalk Labs in Toronto, to Masdar in Abu Dhabi, developments wired with sensors and computers have changed cityscapes and architectural frontiers. And even new cities, like Songdo in South Korea and Konza in Kenya, made of data and algorithms as much as concrete, steel, and glass, have begun to rise from scratch, monuments to the new era of ubiquitous computation.

This conjuncture of corporate interests, scientific efforts, and political tactics made the smart city an over-popular trope and an imperative for urban planning and governance. The idea of smart city is, at once, highly standardised around a set of elements—Internet of Things and automation, efficiency and environmental sustainability—and vague enough to be moulded around different, even conflicting agendas. In India, for example, smart cities have become a key component of the nationalist-neoliberalist programme pursued by the Bharatiya Janata Party (BJP) government led by Narendra Modi. Launched in 2015, the Smart Cities Mission is set to turn 100 Indian cities into smart cities through massive investments in digital infrastructures, as a way to foster economic growth and innovation. For Ayona Datta (2015) the programme fuses India's postcolonial and developmental tradition of urban planning as a modernisation project, with homegrown neoliberalism. Strongly corporate-oriented and explicitly aimed at attracting global investors, the programme prescribes neoliberal measures, such as building public–private partnerships with the tech sector, as conditions for cities to receive funding. In a country where urban inequality is a persistent legacy of colonialism, the Smart Cities Mission has been criticised for ignoring the urban poor issues and for creating even more polarised cities. In Cape Town, the smart city followed a very different script. The Smart City Strategy launched by the City of Cape Town in 2009 has an explicit mission of addressing the urban socio-economic divide inherited by the apartheid. Here, the smart city is represented as a vehicle of social justice through technological innovation. At the same time, however, in parallel and often in cooperation with municipal initiatives, the smart city has been embraced and actively pursued by a coalition of entrepreneurial actors—billionaires, global platforms, startup incubators—which have taken very seriously the idea of turning Cape Town into Africa's digital capital, especially in terms of industrial and commercial leadership.

The risk that smart city projects might be profit-driven and dominated by the corporate sector, resulting in less democratic and more unequal cities, has been a forceful critical argument in recent years. The reliance on data and software for the management of anything urban has been seen as generating new forms of urban technocracy (Kitchin, 2014a; Kitchin et al., 2019), whereby democratic deliberation and policy-making are replaced by a new class of 'experts', and key infrastructures are managed by the corporate sector. For Alberto Vanolo (2014), smart city projects enact a specific governmental strategy, which cultivates forms of citizenship that are compatible with the neoliberalisation of urban governance. By creating specific regimes of visualisation—typically provided by commercial software—smart cities also reduce the complexity of urban life to the abstractions of data and models, thus leaving out anything unsuitable for computation (McNeill, 2015; Mattern, 2021). Moreover, it has been observed that smart cities also provide ideal conditions for tech companies to accumulate, and capitalise on, data (Sadowski, 2020) while enabling novel regimes of labour exploitation (Burns & Welker, 2022). Another important strand of critical work on smart cities has focused on surveillance. Smart cities are predicated upon the extensive extraction of data from all sorts of sources, which are then processed via (more and more automated) algorithms. This means that citizens can be profiled, and potentially discriminated or targeted (Kitchin, 2014b). For David Lyon (2016), smart city projects normalise ubiquitous surveillance as a new urban regime. Murakami Wood and MacKinnon (2019) note that surveillance in smart city projects is oligoptic, insofar as some groups of people, places, and feelings are under intense scrutiny, while others are ignored. These accounts, and many others, have generated awareness around the risks that smart urbanism poses to democracy, social justice, individual and collective freedoms. In so doing, these studies necessarily pointed to broad processes and tendencies. At the same time, work remains to be done to grasp, as accurately as possible, how smart technologies operate in context, producing distinct socio-spatial arrangements and political effects. Surveillance, while critical, is only one aspect of the processes of algorithmic governance. But algorithms do more than monitoring and capturing data: they *produce* something—models, ontologies, worlds. How exactly do predictive and decision models generate new norms, parameters, and modes of existence? Which nodes of knowledge-power, technical procedures, and political and economic agendas define the operational context of those models? What kind of futures and presents are made possible or impossible by these technologies? To answer these questions through examples from New Town Kolkata and Cape Town, this book delves into the ways in which speculation, as a technopolitical force, informs and works through smart city projects.

Why Smart Cities Are Speculative

Smartness is not only a matter of technologies; it is, more significantly, an epistemology of preemption and actionability, 'a way of knowing and representing the world so that one can act in and upon that world' (Halpern & Mitchell, 2023, xi). This epistemology is inherently speculative in that it seeks, at once, to imagine, generate, and capitalise upon the future. The smartness epistemology also materialises in the form of never-ending experiments and perennial testing. In exploring smart cities as speculative projects, I am building upon a wealth of recent studies that tackle the manifold angles and lives of speculation. Speculative urbanism, speculative technologies, speculation as a social logic, speculative ethics, are only some of the diverse research paths that see speculation as a powerful force at work across several critical domains of our everyday life. In recent years, speculative urbanism has emerged as a field of research tackling the ways in which financial networks and real estate capital are reshaping urban planning and governance, especially in the Global South. In world-class city-making projects in Jakarta and Bengaluru, scholars have registered the many and diverse facets through which a wide range of actors, from private equity to rural communities, speculate on urban futures and their place in them (Goldman, 2011; Goldman & Narayan, 2021; Leitner & Sheppard, 2023). Importantly, these works displace speculation from its traditional site of financial investments, to illustrate how it gets to encompass a variety of urban imaginaries and socio-cultural practices across different social sectors (Fields, 2023). Financial operations at different scales are also crucial to my analysis of smart cities as speculative projects. In both New Town and Cape Town, a wide range of financial networks, from massive real estate projects like the Bengal Silicon Valley, to the puzzle of venture capital, angel investors, and startups in Cape Town, is at the core of the smart city. At the same time, in my research I have encountered modes of speculation that closely resemble financial logics, yet go beyond the realm of finance, seeping into urban design and governance. The notion of speculative urbanism that I propose in this book is therefore broader than the established one, and captures three interrelated facets. The first is the politics of experimentation. Smart cities are speculative because they only ever exist as a constellation of experiments, and as the projection of a future form that is never fully achieved. This is what Orit Halpern and colleagues, in their work on Songdo, refer to as testbed urbanism (2013). A greenfield smart city and Special Economic Zone, Songdo is a site of experimentation for the new big data epistemology, for new profit strategies based on data mining, and for a new form of urbanism based on ubiquitous computing. But the experiment never ends. In testbed urbanism, the smart city and all the calculative infrastructures within it become an engine for growth that cannot stop; rather, it is set to continually exceed its technical limits. And if massive experiments like Songdo offer striking examples, testbeds can be found at any scale. Smart systems are continually tuned, amended, and updated. From greenfield projects to retrofitting and all the possible combinations in between, smart cities in the making are all recursive testbeds, which are never meant to settle into a definitive form. In both New Town and Cape Town, I found that what generates novel forms of governmentality, value, and life is not the final accomplishment of a fully formed new city. It is rather the continuous work in progress, the experiments and trials. Although the smart city of New Town is clearly still far from materialising, and in fact, it may never, it has in the meantime restructured urban governance, shaped new lifestyles, and triggered a new wave of economic operations, from delivery platforms starting business in the township, to massive real estate developments like the Bengal Silicon Valley. 'Africa's smartest city', the 'Digital Gateway to Africa, or the 'Silicon Cape' are some of the powerful narratives within which, over the past few years, an ecosystem of finance and tech companies has emerged, neighbourhoods have been gentrified, and key sectors of urban governance have been turned into platforms. Importantly, these experiments have a spatial impact. Rather than fulfilling the promise of holistic, seamlessly interconnected urban environments, 'smart' city experiments fragment and hierarchise the urban space. As Chapter 2 illustrates, the tests and trials of digital infrastructures tend to concentrate in specific zones of the city—wealthier neighbourhoods or business hubs—reproducing long-standing patterns of socio-spatial inequality. In New Town, for example, business parks equipped with advanced technologies, and highly securitised, stand alongside slums that lack running water or sewerage. Smart infrastructures are trialled only in selected areas of the city, while the rest lag behind, sometimes deprived of even basic services. In Cape Town, the wealthier and wither parts of the city teem with all things 'smart'—technologies, app-based services, startups, incubators, etc. Much less so in the apartheid townships, which are nevertheless testbeds for cultivating forms of digital entrepreneurship, as well as for tech-based activism for below. As a result, and as I have argued in previous work, smart experiments operate as bordering processes, which intersect and even magnify existing inequalities (Antenucci, 2021).

While endlessly evoking an indefinite future, smart experiments also need to be made actionable, and profitable, in the present. This is the second facet of speculation in smart cities, which concerns the inner logic of the computing techniques that generate models of future possibilities and shape decisions in the present. Turning urban data into models of the future, to enable anticipatory governance, is a pillar of smart city projects. In this book, I look specifically at algorithms and platforms for urban security. Over the past two decades or so, platforms have evolved into pivotal urban architecture, mediating and reconfiguring relations around an expanding range of activities, services, and commodities (Barns, 2020; Lezcynski, 2019). While the majority of literature on

10   I. ANTENUCCI

platform urbanism focuses on corporate platforms, the security platforms that I examine in this book are examples of public–private partnerships. Customised software is provided and maintained by private providers, but the platform is operated by departments of the municipal administration. In New Town Kolkata, software for social media monitoring has been tested that promises to enable authorities to detect potential threats or disruptions of various kinds—from environmental hazards, to discontent among citizens—and to act preemptively. In Cape Town, the Emergency Policing and Incident Command (EPIC) is a platform designed to optimise emergency response by sorting incidents into different categories and producing risk alerts. Both platforms rely on predictive analytics to model a wide range of future scenarios, detect threats, and make decisions. As Louise Amoore noted, a speculative logic is mathematically built into the Bayesian inferences that underpin many predictive algorithms, wherein a set of unknown values become visible and meaningful only when associated with each other, and where formulae resemble 'if and, in association with, then' (Amoore, 2013, p. 59). The asterisks are replaced with events, names, and possible threats based not on facts but on the inner rules of algorithmic inferences. For Claudia Aradau (2015), the different families of algorithms operating in urban management software and control rooms are closer to 'mathematical divination' than to science, as they tend to formulate hypotheses rather than provide factual evidence. But no matter how speculative, algorithmic predictions are also inherently normative. Designed for the sake of decision-making, analytics arrange the unintelligible mass of data into models of the future that are actionable in the present. In so doing, they generate orders and configurations of the world that are inherently political. In recent years, a rich scholarship has made clear how the algorithms at work in information, policing, finance and banking, education, labour management, social security, and so on, are neither objective nor neutral, but shaped by ideologies, prejudices, and agendas (see, among others, Benjamin, 2019; Eubanks, 2018; Noble, 2018; O'Neill, 2016). As they are entrusted with making decisions about anything from organising content on the Internet to predicting crime in a given neighbourhood, algorithms reproduce and, literally, encode racism, gender, and class discrimination into everyday life. Not only are analytics biased and politically performative: They are also highly abstract and, often, self-referential. As data scientist Cathy O'Neill (2016) illustrates, algorithms incorporate blind spots (aspects that are deliberately ignored); use data proxies to fill in for the lack of authentic data; and legitimate themselves via a feedback loop that, all too often, has no ties with the real life of people and things. As O'Neill bluntly puts it, algorithmic systems 'define their own reality and use it to justify their results. This type of model is self-perpetuating, highly destructive—and very common' (2016, p. 16).

As 'smart' security technologies are implemented in urban environments, they incorporate and act upon pre-existing conditions of inequality and discrimination. Writing about facial recognition and geographical information systems (GIS) in their early days, Stephen Graham (2005) warned us that software *sorts* the city and (re)configures social and power relations. Today, as computing systems grow in power and pervasiveness, the need to unpack the algorithmic operations that increasingly govern urban life is becoming even more pressing. In her book *The Politics of Possibility*, Louise Amoore (2013) explains how security decisions are no longer informed by strict probability, 'by the deductive proving or disproving of scientific and statistical data but by the inductive incorporation of suspicion, imagination, and preemption' (2013, p. 10). In Foucauldian terms, preemption is a modality of intervention in the milieu, not meant to stop single events, but to (re)arrange the elements in order to influence the unfolding of future events. Under this perspective, 'facts' (or whatever was agreed to be considered facts), as a basis for decisions and actions, are replaced by algorithmic models. As Marieke de Goede writes in her study of the pursuit of terrorist money following the terrorist attacks of 9/11 (2012), security works speculatively because security decisions can only be made once a specific 'visual field', populated with threats and enemies, is created and mobilised. Translating this concept into urban context, one needs to ask what kind of visual and discursive fields underpin the production of security systems and decisions. Looking at experiments with smart security in New Town Kolkata and Cape Town, I ask how algorithmic speculations incorporate situated imaginaries of risk and insecurity, while acting upon material conditions of inequality and marginalisation. I also interrogate the ways in which new technologies for urban security produce novel ways of knowing and understanding the city, as well as new parameters of citizenship.

Finally, smart cities are speculative in the proper financial sense. Financial operations are the lifeblood of smart city projects at any scale. From tech startups to real estate investors, a broad spectrum of financial actors are drawn to speculate on the city to come. For Lisa Adkins (2018), speculation in today's world has become not only the primary mode of capitalist accumulation, but a system of social organisation. The proliferation of mundane forms of debt, and the (speculative) calculation of the possibilities of future repayment impose a distinct temporal regime on the lives of individuals and households. The same logic can be seen at work in smart cities, where much of the economic landscape, from large infrastructural projects to startups and commercial platforms, moves at the pace of financial capital. In New Town Kolkata, the announcements and plans for the smart city to come were sufficient to resurrect investments at any scale, from developers resuming construction in unfinished complexes to sales of residential and commercial spaces picking up again, to platforms like Uber starting operations in the area. In Cape Town, a cohort of entrepreneurs and investors has catalysed flows of venture capital and startups, turning the city into a regional hub for financial and technological speculations. Importantly, these speculative operations *in* and *on* smart cities do not come out of thin air, but are grafted upon urban histories of violence and dispossession. This book traces the genealogies of land grabbing and gentrification—from the displacement of Rajarhat's rural communities, to the evictions of residents from the Woodstock neighbourhood in Cape Town—on which smart cities, and the financial speculations associated with them, are built.

Besides, speculations proliferate across the growing number of commercial platforms that offer services such as food delivery or transport, and which settle in smart cities as favourable business environments. These platforms, such as Uber, are at the forefront of speculation: Fuelled by rounds of fundraising from private equity, they operate within the horizon of the stock market. At the same time, critical to these platforms are the same techniques of algorithmic modelling, and the same drive to predict and appropriate the future, which platforms for urban government rely upon. As De Goede (2012) observes, in both the domains of security and finance, the future is a terrain that needs to be colonised in order to gain profit, be it in the form of money or political control. Platforms are at once objects and subjects of speculation: objects, in that they respond to investors and to the command of financial markets; and subjects, in that modelling urban data to predict future or even real-time scenarios and optimise their operations is at the core of their business model. Speculative and extractive technologies are therefore allied and entangled. Commercial platforms use predictive analytics to maximise the extraction of value from the whole spectrum of their urban operations. Take for example how a food delivery platform works.

1 INTRODUCTION   13

Riders (those who deliver meals to customers) are monitored, scored, and disciplined through performance indicators. Customers are profiled and targeted with customised advertising to make them buy more. And the city as a whole, from the weather to public events, is scrutinised for more commercial opportunities. At the same time, what happens at the level of financial markets affects the extractive processes 'on the ground'. For example, if investors demand returns from a company that has been running at loss for long, algorithmic pressure on workers intensifies, and their income plummets. In other words, in the operations of commercial platforms in smart cities, speculation and extraction coexist and feed each other. If extractive practices, powered by data mining and predictive models, are inscribed into a broader horizon of speculation, then speculative operations are fuelled by maximising extraction from the urban environment.

The Unlikely Smart Cities

Neither of the two cities narrated in this book has much to do with the mainstream representation of a smart city. They don't meet most of the common smart city standards and they don't top global smart city rankings. Both cities are in the Global South and both are still coming to terms, albeit in different ways, with the legacy of their colonial pasts. At the same time, both cities are strongly committed, both financially and politically, to digital technologies as a potential solution to urban problems and as a 'worlding' strategy. In fact, global models of urbanisation and technologies in New Town Kolkata and Cape Town are faced with local histories of inequality and segregation, as well as with homegrown urban agendas. This results in configurations of space, government, and economies, which are at once inherently global, and irreducibly contingent.

For Ishita Dey, Ranabir Samaddar, and Suhit K. Sen, who wrote a thoroughly researched book on the making of New Town Kolkata (2013), the new town must be understood first and foremost in its *otherness* to the old city. Crucial to the rise and fall of the British empire, and later to become almost a synonym for urban disaster, for decades Kolkata has been also a laboratory of postcolonial thinking and debates on capitalist development, modernity, and governmentality. As much as Kolkata was the ungovernable city of intellectual communities and political mobilisation, heritage and inequality, so New Town was meant to be its opposite: a flat, sanitised space, planned for the convenience of corporate operations and for the comfort of the middle-class. Yet the project was pursued by grabbing the lands and destroying the livelihoods of local communities, that is, as Dey et al. observe, by reiterating practices of primitive accumulation. For Kanyal Sanyal (2007), the constant repetition of primitive accumulation is one of the defining conditions of postcolonial capitalism, resulting in the production of a surplus population that is not absorbed in the capitalist system as waged labour, but lives on its margins as informal economy—in Sanyal's words, subsistence or need economy. The management of these forms of poverty, as attempts to mitigate the effects of the recursive violence of primitive accumulation on the lives of the dispossessed, are what defines postcolonial governmentality for Sanyal. Writing about New Town Kolkata, Sanyal and Bhatthacharya (2011) stress how primitive accumulation generated a local need economy that needs to negotiate its conditions of existence and reproduction under the perennial threat of eviction. This is the same terrain where Partha Chatterjee (2004) situates the 'political society': the dispossessed that only through endless negotiations and mobilisations can affirm—if only precariously—their needs and rights, which would otherwise not be granted by the legal framework. In New Town Kolkata, for example, Chatterjee notes that some expropriated land owners were able to negotiate their resettlement and compensation by making claims and rallying collectively. For Dey and colleagues, on the other hand, in this particular case, the violence of accumulation was beyond management and could not be reabsorbed within a governmental framework. Rather, this violence produced an excess that manifested in various forms of struggle—from physical confrontation and sabotage to legal battles—and which still disrupts the development of the township (Dey et al., 2013).

Abdoumaliq Simone (2001) argues that colonial urbanism shaped cities so they would act on bodies and social formations (p. 18) in order to maintain relations of subalternity. Significantly, not only is this logic still tangible in old colonial cities, it also haunts new urban projects like New Town Kolkata. If the old colonial city was deliberately segregated on the basis of race and nationality—like the White and Black towns of Calcutta under British rule—the new postcolonial city is informally, but deeply divided along class and cast lines. In New Town, the slums that stretch next to corporate buildings and shopping malls materialise the heterogeneity of the postcolonial (urban) condition, where advanced capitalism and need economies, privilege and destitution, civil rights and political society coexist in uneasy and unstable relations. Yet, following Ahiwa Ong and Ananya Roy (2011), there is much more to postcolonial cities than the narrative of slums and poverty. A wealth of 'worlding' strategies unfold across economies and urban expansion, and the smart city, with all its controversies, is one of them. The Indian Smart Cities Mission (SCM) programme allocated ₹980 billion (approximately USD15 billion) to the improvement, redevelopment, and extension of 109 cities across the country. Cities had to compete against each other for funding by submitting projects for new infrastructures and urban remaking. The municipalities hired global consultants to put together successful applications. For example, the New Town Kolkata Development Authority wrote its bid with the UK firm Future Cities Catapult, and was among the winning cities, in 2016. The Smart City Mission appeared to be a priority for Modi's government, which had been crafting its own mix of nationalism and neoliberalism—combining corporate-oriented policies with narratives of Great India and religious extremism—since it came to office in 2014. Smart urbanism was framed as a way of attracting foreign investors and advancing India's position in global economic networks, while supporting homegrown capitalism at the same time. Both domestic and multinational companies, including major Indian holdings Tata, Infosys, and the Mahindra Group, big tech players like Oracle, IBM, Cisco, and Google, and global consultants such as Accenture, have been involved in designing the pathway to the smart city. They organised business conferences and workshops, provided consultancies, and sponsored projects. Many of these companies settled down in New Town well before the launch of smart city projects, benefiting from the Special Economic Zones policies of the past two decades. In fact, the whole township of New Town was planned during the 1990s, as a Special Economic Zone for the IT industry, with some residential and commercial developments attached, by the Left Front government of West Bengal then in power. Aggressively pursued but scarcely successful, the zoning policy left behind displaced farmers and destitute communities, without generating the promised results in terms of employment, development, and collective wealth. By the time New Town applied for government funding, the place was an inconsistent agglomeration of unfinished flyovers and luxury hotels, corporate enclaves and unsold condos, upscale shopping malls, and bustees.

In Cape Town, four centuries of colonial rule were followed by five decades of a homegrown apartheid regime. In the post-apartheid context, the enduring legacies of colonisation merge with the effects of the systemic segregation and economic marginalisation of the black and coloured population. As Achille Mbembe (2015) writes, twenty years after the end of apartheid, formal equality before the law corresponds to sharp inequalities—social, spatial, and economic—between blacks and whites. 'The white propertied class', says Mbembe, has not lost its structural privilege. They may have lost their political power, but 'they did not die as a class' (p. 11) and, as a class, they actively engage in relegating racism to the past, refusing to acknowledge racial segregation as a persisting cause of inequality between blacks and whites. Post-apartheid politics have taken shape, over the past two decades, around the imperative to overcome structural inequalities, poverty, and racial divides. Yet this agenda has generated ambiguous instruments and results. Andries Du Toit (2012) notes how, after the end of apartheid, pro-poor policies, such as the significant redistributive expenditures for infrastructures, service provisions, and social welfare payments, benefited from wide consensus among South African political forces and society. However, poverty discourses are typically articulated in ways that tend to depoliticise poverty by disconnecting its causes from sedimented inequalities and social conflicts, and by overlooking the agency of the poor. In post-apartheid politics, Du Toit explains, the government of poverty is a political project, which seeks 'to ameliorate and contain its worst political and social effects, while stopping short of challenging the social processes and arrangements that perpetuate and entrench it' (Du Toit, 2012, p. 6). Furthermore, pro-poor policies are part of a political contract whereby the provisioning of resources towards specific groups secures the grounds of power to political organisations. For James Ferguson (2015), distributive, pro-poor measures—such as cash transfers to low-income individuals—have become embedded in a neoliberal narrative according to which this money would empower individuals to enter the market as entrepreneurial actors. More generally, the promotion of entrepreneurialism as a strategy to ensure economic growth and social justice, is a defining element of post-apartheid governmentality. Various technologies of poverty management have been experimented with, especially in the townships, at the intersections between NGOs, entrepreneurial incubators, and microfinance (Roy, 2011; Pollio, 2019). Concurrently, aggressive dynamics of urban accumulation have constantly manifested in the enclosure of public spaces and in the gentrification of former low-income neighbourhoods that mark Cape Town's attempts to meet world-class standards and position itself as a node of global circuits of capital. For David McDonald (2012), post-apartheid Cape Town has been redesigned as a site of capitalist accumulation, within a neoliberal framework that reproduces and reinforces existing patterns of economic and racial divide. The transformation of Cape Town into a smart city condenses the fluctuation and tensions of post-apartheid politics between a social justice agenda—albeit declined in entrepreneurial forms—and capitalist strategies. The smart city was originally embraced by the City of Cape Town as a framework for generating economic inclusion and social justice, and for dealing with the urban legacy of apartheid. Institutional discourses present smartness as a solution to expand access to education, create jobs, improve public services, and, ultimately, to democratise urban life. At the same time, the smart city carries on the capitalist vision of a 'Silicon Cape'—an African hub for tech startups and the IT industry. The creation of digital infrastructures and tech hubs is a catalyst for venture capital and commercial platforms, which see the smart city as a business opportunity.

The Smart City Strategy for Cape Town was launched in 2000 by Unicity, the then recently formed, unified city government. In the first stage of the project, known as Smart Cape Access and launched in 2002 in partnership with IT companies Xerox and CableCom Ltd., free computer and internet access was provided to public libraries in disadvantaged areas. In 2009, the city started rolling out broadband fibre networks throughout the metropolitan area and building a platform for e-governance, with an estimated investment of R 1.7 billion (approximately USD 1.3 billion). The development of IT infrastructures brought in private actors as well. In 2014, the city signed lease agreements with eight service providers, which took over portions of the fibre networks, with a commitment to extend connectivity to the poorer areas of the city. In 2013, a booklet titled *Digital Gateway to Africa*, jointly authored by the City of Cape Town, business forum Accelerate Cape Town, Wesgro (the government agency for tourism, trade, and investment in Cape Town and the Western Cape) and global consultant PWC, presented Cape Town as the African Silicon Valley. The publication emphasised numerous reasons for investing in the local IT sector, such as a young and thriving entrepreneurial scene, business-friendly governance, a strong financial sector, excellent universities, and, not least, a beautiful place to live. In the same year, IBM included Cape Town in its Smart Cities Challenge—a consultancy programme intended to redesign urban governance through data and software—and sent a team of consultants to advise the local administration on how to effectively manage its social assets and optimise service delivery. In all of this, the spatial distribution of urban infrastructures, shaped by racial segregation, remained largely unchanged and deeply unequal. In contrast to the central, wealthier, and whither areas of the city, the townships remained largely underserviced of both basic and digital infrastructures. As Nancy Odendaal (2016) observes, Cape Town's smart city has become a field of intersection and tensions between a developmental agenda, strongly pursued by governments and corporate players on one side, and digital activism 'from below' on the other. Despite limited access, smart technologies have become an instrument of organisation and mobilisation for activists, such as the Social Justice Coalition, that use social media to campaign for township communities (Odendaal, 2016).

In both New Town Kolkata and Cape Town, smart city projects have taken shape amidst contradictions—between global aspirations and home-grown politics, capitalist accumulation and dispossession, poverty relief, and persistent inequality. In both cities, digitalisation is not a linear transition to an advanced stage of development, as commercial and political narratives often suggest. Nor it is the mere local reception of a global model. Rather, the making of smart cities is an uneven, disruptive process, where different regimes of time, space, and urbanism, merge and collide. This book describes how these tensions play out across the speculative infrastructures, technologies and economies of smart cities.

SPECULATION AS METHOD

One major challenge that I faced in the course of this research was that many of the projects and technologies I am writing about did not yet exist—at least, not in their full form—at the time of writing. Most of the time, I was looking into something that was in the making or even completely abstract. Some projects only existed on paper, others were under construction, and others were being tested and trialled. The effects of these infrastructures, objects, and systems on the urban environment were still very much indeterminate and not always clearly observable. The planned, the unfinished, and the testing became my primary research objects.

Speculation is the key concept of this book, and defines the logics and forces at work in the making of smart cities. But speculation(s) also turned out to be a key research method, shaped by my encounters with an array of empirical and theoretical situations. The concept of speculation captures the tension between visions and projects of the future, and the operations that seek not only to materialise those futures but also to make them actionable in the present. It is a tension that is immediately generative of effects. The security calculations and financial initiatives discussed in this book are fuelled by precisely that imperative to appropriate unknown possibilities. Smart city projects seek to capture urban futures and to project onto them distinct visions of the built environment, social interactions, government, and economy. As such, these projects are constitutively unfinished, experimental, and speculative. The fact that something does not exist in its—supposedly—final form does not mean it does not exist at all. On the contrary, projects and plans live their own existence, which is full of economic, social, and political effects. As Jennifer Gabrys suggests (2016), planning documents and experiments are speculative, because they not only represent specific configurations of the future but also produce them in the present, by enabling and shaping practices, norms, decisions, and investments. Smart cities are testbeds, in which continuous experiments become the very terrain of governance and economies. Researching speculations and testbeds means looking at provisional configurations of materials, protocols, and strategies, which are open to multiple outcomes and effects and which are in a state of continuous update. It also means trying to understand their performative effects across unstable temporalities, where the boundaries between present and future, facts and projections are always blurred. Challenges and questions remain: how can speculative processes be examined in practice and assessed? How can the effects of infrastructures that have not yet been fully materialised be documented? These questions shaped my research, both conceptually and practically, as I tried to chart the continuous echoes and links between projects, experiments, examples, expectations, decisions, and effects (where possible). These non-linear relations between different elements and time regimes are constitutive of urban processes (economic, social, and political) and techniques of government alike. To investigate them, I drew upon several ethnographic scholarships, including various declinations of the ethnography of circulation and of the 'follow the thing' approach (among others, Marcus, 1995; and Parks & Starosielski, 2015; Tsing, 2011); Susan

Leigh Star's (1999) ethnography of infrastructure; relational ethnography (Desmond, 2014); and the nonlocal ethnography suggested by Gregory Feldman (2011a, 2011b) for the study of global apparatuses. The latter in particular questions the 'empiricist anxiety' that often affects ethnographic research, providing a methodological route for studying 'relations between disconnected actors through abstract mediating agents' (2011a, p. 378). The field of this research is a milieu made of humans, machines, code, hardware, discourses, and more. Herein, my research 'objects' are in fact the processes through which smart infrastructures are discursively and materially assembled, tested, and updated; and through which they speculatively govern, and capitalise on, the city. To research these processes, I spent time in the field, followed objects, documented narratives, traced infrastructures, and drew, in general, on a set of practices that belong to the ethnographic tradition. At the same time, however, elements of the processes that I investigated continuously evaded, and/ or exceeded the boundary of observation and personal experience. Scale, distance, secrecy, incompleteness, and technical impenetrability were only some of the reasons why some infrastructures could not always—and not entirely—be researched through personal experience. Some crucial nodes—think of the offices where software engineers and data scientists set up and update platforms, such as SAP HANA or Uber—were physically inaccessible, but crucial to determining urban operations. Moreover, not all the relations that shape the making of smart cities could be fully understood 'in the field'—for example, the financial networks that run throughout smart city projects, in multiple forms—yet examining them was key to understanding the economic stakes in the process. To grasp these complex, stratified relations, I drew on the analysis of a wide range of resources—planning and policy documents, media reports, corporate brochures, advertising material, and technical tutorials—that are not immediately connected in time and space, but which contribute, in different forms, to articulating the processes of urban digitalisation and the operations of government and value extraction. Looking back, I can see my research methods unfolding not as a consistent framework, but rather as a 'bricolage' (Aradau et al., 2014) of concepts and practices shaped by the encounter with work-in-progress, unfinished, and generative research 'objects'. With Aradau and colleagues, I don't see methods as a bridge between theory and practice, but rather as contingent tools that help relate what is usually unrelated, and open novel angles of knowledge. As I delved into speculative forces, my methods turned speculative too: not bound to produce systemic knowledge, but striving to grasp what might be happening at the intersection of future and present.

OUTLINE OF THE CHAPTERS

Chapter 1, *Speculative Urbanism: Transforming the Present Through the Future,* reviews the histories and the unfolding of smart city projects in Kolkata and Cape Town. The chapter explores the projects and narratives through which specific urban futures are constructed and projected onto the present. While their final form remains uncertain or ambiguous, smart city projects and narratives are nevertheless mobilised to manage the present, in terms of both governance and economic practices. In New Town Kolkata, city administrators, real estate players, and financial investors place their stakes on smart city projects (and on the government funding attached to them) to resurrect the fortunes of a failing township development. In parallel, the race to make Cape Town the leading tech hub of Africa shapes urban and regional political strategies while catalysing platforms, startups, and venture capital. Drawing on these examples, I propose an expanded notion of 'speculative urbanism'. Beyond financial operations, which remain crucial, speculative urbanism also registers the strategies of urban statecraft that are enmeshed in smart city projects, as well as the manifold ways in which socio-technical imaginaries of future cities are activated to rule and transform the present.

Chapter 2, *Testbed Cities,* examines the experiments with smart technologies that have been conducted in Cape Town and New Town Kolkata. In Cape Town, the implementation of SAP Enterprise Resource planning (ERP) software for managing city services and business processes has taken shape through tests and trials over a decade. This computing architecture has been leveraged during the 2017/2018 drought, not only to optimise water management but also to induce behavioural changes among urban dwellers. In New Town, experiments with drone surveillance for urban safety and security have ended up targeting street vendors and informal dwellers, who are accused of obstructing urban circulation and disrupting the 'smart' aesthetic of the city. Engaging with recent literature on urban testbeds and testing, the chapter argues that the continuous experiments are themselves a specific form of governance of the smart city. While the outcomes of the technological experiments remain undetermined, the testing processes sediment new modes of being in the city and acting as citizenship, configure new regimes of perception and attentiveness, and establish new political rationalities based on data modelling.

Chapter 3, *Futures and Failures: How Speculative Algorithms (Try to) Run the City*, continues the analysis of smart experiments in Cape and New Town Kolkata. Computing technologies promise that the city can be governed by anticipating and acting upon the future. By exploring platforms for urban security—monitoring citizens' opinions on social media in New Town, and modelling risk scenarios for emergency response in Cape Town—this chapter shows how speculation becomes a distinct technique of urban governmentality. Indeed, the algorithmic modelling and the preemption of future scenarios produce thresholds and parameters, i.e. of what is alarming or dangerous, which generate distinct ontologies of the city and its problems. More than that, it also generates security decisions and new norms. In conversation with critical studies of data and algorithms, the chapter illustrates how algorithmic models often feature built-in bias and flaws related to race, gender, and class, thus potentially magnifying existing patterns of discrimination in urban governance, or even creating novel ones.

Chapter 4, *From Land to Data: Money in the Smart City*, moves on to explore another side of speculative urbanism: how speculation—both financial and technological—and extractivism are aligned in smart city economies. First, the chapter looks into the entanglement of zoning policies, displacement of local communities, and financial ventures, which preceded and unfolded along the making of smart cities in New Town Kolkata and Cape Town. The chapter then brings the focus on the operations of commercial platforms, such as Uber and Zomato, which rely on algorithmic modelling for several purposes, i.e. optimising logistics and monitoring workers' performances, profiling customers, and generating targeted advertising. In these operations, the same speculative techniques that shape urban governance become tools for extracting value from platform workers and customers, as well as from the urban environment as a whole. At the same time, the chapter points out how platforms' operations in urban environments are closely linked to the broader financial strategies of investors and platform stakeholders.

Chapter 5, *Beyond the Smart City: Speculating Otherwise*, wraps up the insights offered by this book, and invites to look ahead. If the smart city framework might be already obsolete, urban speculations are still very much alive, and critical to the operations of powerful platforms like Amazon. But, to conclude this book, the chapter also looks at the other side of speculation, presenting some radical proposals for staying with algorithms and rethinking digital cities for equality, freedom, and social justice. From legal frameworks for technological sovereignty, to practices of hacking and the creation of autonomous digital infrastructures, there is space to reclaim the city even in the age of AI.

References

Adkins, L. (2018). *The time of money*. Stanford University Press.

Amoore, L. (2013). *The politics of possibility: Risk and security beyond probability.* Duke University Press.

Antenucci, I. (2021). Smart cities, smart borders: Sensing networks and security in the urban space. In N. Witjes, N. Pöchhacker, & G. Bowker (Eds.), *Sensing In/Security: Sensors and the making of transnational security infrastructures.* Mattering Press.

Aradau, C. (2015). The signature of security: Big data, anticipation, surveillance. *European Journal of Social Theory, 18*(3), 375–391.

Aradau, C., Huysmans, J., Neal, A., & Voelkner, N. (2014). *Critical security methods: New frameworks for analysis*. Routledge.

Barns, S. (2020). *Platform urbanism: Negotiating platform ecosystems in connected cities*. Palgrave MacMillan.

Benjamin, R. (2019). *Race after technology: Abolitionist tools for the new Jim code.* Polity Press.

Bhatthacharya, R., & Sanyal, K. (2011). Bypassing the squalor: New towns, immaterial labour and exclusion in post-colonial urbanisation. *Economic and Political Weekly, 46*(31), 41–48. http://www.jstor.org/stable/23017875

Burns, R., & Welker, M. (2022). *The logics of surveillance infrastructure: The politics of big data in the global south*. Indiana University Press.

Chatterjee, P. (2004). *The politics of the governed: Reflections on popular politics in most of the world*. Columbia University Press.

Cirolia, L. R., Sitas, R., Pollio, A., Sebarenzi, A. G., & Guma, P. K. (2023). Silicon Savannahs and motorcycle taxis: A Southern perspective on the frontiers of platform urbanism. *Environment and Planning a: Economy and Space, 55*(8), 1989–2008.

Datta, A. (2015). New urban utopias of postcolonial India: 'Entrepreneurial urbanization' in Dholera smart city, Gujarat. *Dialogues in Human Geography, 5*(1), 3–22.

Datta, A., & Shaban, A. (Eds.). (2023). *Mega-urbanization in the Global South: Fast cities and new urban utopias of the postcolonial state*. Routledge.

Dey, I., Samaddar, R., & Sen, S. K. (2013). *Beyond Kolkata: Rajarhat and the dystopia of urban imagination*. Routledge India.

24   I. ANTENUCCI

De Goede, M. (2012). *Speculative security: The politics of pursuing terrorist monies*. University of Minnesota Press.

Desmond, M. (2014). Relational ethnography. *Theory and Society, 43*(5), 547–579.

Du Toit, A. (2012). The trouble with poverty: Reflections on South Africa's post—apartheid anti–poverty consensus. Working Paper no. 22. *PLAAS*. University of the Western Cape.

Easterling, K. (2014). *Extrastatecraft: The power of infrastructure space*. Verso Books.

Edensor, T., & Jayne, M. (Eds.). (2011). *Urban theory beyond the West: A world of cities*. Routledge.

Eubanks, V. (2018). *Automating inequality: How high-tech tools profile, police, and punish the poor*. Martin's Press.

Feldman, G. (2011). *The migration apparatus: Security, labor, and policymaking in the European Union*. Stanford University Press.

Feldman, G. (2011). If ethnography is more than participant-observation, then relations are more than connections: The case for nonlocal ethnography in a world of apparatuses. *Anthropological Theory, 11*(4), 375–395.

Ferguson, J. (2010). The uses of neoliberalism. *Antipode, 41*, 166–184.

Ferguson, J. (2015). *Give a man a fish: Reflections on the new politics of distribution*. Duke University Press.

Fields, D. (2023). Speculative urbanism. *Environment and Planning A: Economy and Space, 55*(2), 511–516.

Gabrys, J. (2016). *Program earth: Environmental sensing technology and the making of a computational planet*. University of Minnesota Press.

Galdon-Clavell, G. (2013). (Not so) smart cities?: The drivers, impact and risks of surveillance-enabled smart environments. *Science and Public Policy, 40*(6), 717–723.

Goldman, M. (2011). Speculative urbanism and the making of the next world city. *International Journal of Urban and Regional Research, 35*(3), 555–581.

Goldman, M., & Narayan, D. (2021). Through the Optics of Finance: Speculative Urbanism and the Transformation of Markets. *International Journal of Urban and Regional Research, 45*(2), 209–231.

Graham, S. D. (2005). Software-sorted geographies. *Progress in Human Geography, 29*(5), 562–580.

Halpern, O., & Mitchell, R. (2023). *The Smartness Mandate*. MIT Press.

Hollands, R. G. (2015). Critical interventions into the corporate smart city. *Cambridge Journal of Regions, Economy and Society, 8*(1), 61–77.

Kitchin, R. (2014a). *The data revolution: Big data, open data, data infrastructures and their consequences*. SAGE Publications.

Kitchin, R. (2014b). The real-time city? Big data and smart urbanism. *GeoJournal, 79*(1), 1–14.

Kitchin, R., & Perng, S.-Y. (2016). *Code and the city.* Routledge.

Kitchin, R., Cardullo, P., & Di Feliciantonio, C. (2019). *The right to the smart city.* Emerald Publishing Limited.

Leitner, H., & Sheppard, E. (2023). Unleashing speculative urbanism: Speculation and urban transformations. *Environment and Planning a: Economy and Space, 55*(2), 359–366.

Leszczynski, A. (2019). Glitchy vignettes of platform urbanism. *Environment and Planning D: Society and Space, 37*(6), 1001–1019.

Lyon, D. (2016). Surveillance, Snowden, and big data: Capacities, consequences, critique. *Big Data & Society, 3*(2), 1–13.

Marcus, G. E. (1995). Ethnography in/of the world system: The emergence of multi-sited ethnography. *Annual Review of Anthropology, 24,* 95–117.

Mattern, S. (2021). *A city is not a computer: Other urban intelligences.* Princeton University Press.

Melgaço, L., & Van Brakel, R. (2021). Counter-surveillance and alternative epistemologies in the smart city. *Surveillance & Society, 19*(2), 161–167.

Mbembe, A. (2015). Decolonizing knowledge and the question of the archive. *Public lecture at the Wits Institute for Social and Economic Research (WISER),* University of the Witwatersrand.

McDonald, D. A. (2012). *World city syndrome: Neoliberalism and inequality in Cape Town.* Routledge.

McNeill, D. (2015). Global firms and smart technologies: IBM and the reduction of cities. *Transactions of the Institute of British Geographers, 40*(4), 562–574.

Monahan, T. (2018). The image of the smart city: Surveillance protocols and social inequality. In Y. Watanabe (Ed.), *Handbook of Cultural Security* (pp. 210–226). Edward Elgar.

Murakami Wood, D., & Mackinnon, D. (2019). Partial platforms and oligoptic surveillance in the smart city. *Surveillance & Society, 17*(1/2), 176–182.

Noble, S. U. (2018). *Algorithms of oppression: How search engines reinforce racism.* NYU Press

Odendaal, N. (2016). Getting smart about smart cities in Cape Town. In S. Marvin, A. Luque-Ayala, & C. McFarlane (Eds.), *Smart urbanism: Utopian vision or false dawn* (pp. 71–87). Routledge.

Offenhuber, D., & Ratti, C. (2014). *Decoding the city: Urbanism in the age of big data.* Birkhäuser.

O'Neill, C. (2016). *Weapons of math destruction: How big data increases inequality and threatens democracy.* Crown Books.

Parks, L., & Starosielski, N. (Eds.). (2015). *Signal traffic: Critical studies of media infrastructures.* University of Illinois Press.

Parnell, S., & Robinson, J. (2013). (Re)theorizing cities from the Global South: Looking beyond neoliberalism. *Urban Geography, 33*(4), 593–617.

26   I. ANTENUCCI

Perng, S.-Y., & Maalsen, S. (2020). Civic infrastructure and the appropriation of the smart city. *Urban Studies, 57*(14), 2862–2878.

Pollio, A. (2019). Forefronts of the sharing economy: Uber in Cape Town. *International Journal of Urban and Regional Research, 43*(4), 760–775.

Pollio, A. (2020). Making the silicon cape of Africa: Tales, theories and the narration of startup urbanism. *Urban Studies, 57*(13), 2715–2732.

Roy, A., & Ong, A. (Eds.). (2011). *Worlding cities: Asian experiments and the art of being global.* Wiley-Blackwell.

Sadowski, J., & Bendor, R. (2019). Selling smartness: Corporate narratives and the smart city as a sociotechnical imaginary. *Science, Technology, & Human Values, 44*(3), 540–563.

Sanyal, K. (2007). *Rethinking capitalist development: Primitive accumulation, governmentality and post-colonial capitalism.* Routledge.

Savini, F., & Raco, M. (2021). *Planning and knowledge: How new forms of technocracy are shaping contemporary cities.* Policy Press.

Simone, A. (2001). On the Worlding of African Cities. *African Studies Review, 44*(2), 15–41.

Söderström, O., Paasche, T., & Klauser, F. (2014). Smart cities as corporate storytelling. *City, 18*(3), 307–320.

Söderström, O., Mermet, A.-C., & Hanakata, N. (2020). Smart cities: From utopia to dystopia. In M. Gunder, A. Madanipour, & V. Watson (Eds.), *The Routledge handbook of planning theory* (pp. 396–407). Routledge.

Star, S. L. (1999). The ethnography of infrastructure. *American Behavioral Scientist, 43*(3), 377–391.

Townsend, A. M. (2015). *Smart cities: Big data, civic hackers, and the quest for a new utopia.* W.W. Norton & Company.

Tsing, A. L. (2011). *Friction: An ethnography of global connection.* Princeton University Press.

Vanolo, A. (2014). Smartmentality: The smart city as disciplinary strategy. *Urban Studies, 51*(5), 883–898.

Van Dijck, J. (2014). Datafication, dataism, and dataveillance: Big data between scientific paradigm and ideology. *Surveillance & Society, 12*(2), 197–208.

CHAPTER 2

Speculative Urbanism: Transforming the Present Through the Future

In 2016, with a dramatic move, the Chief Minister of West Bengal and leader of the Trinamool Congress, Mamata Banerjee, decided to withdraw New Town Kolkata from the Smart Cities Mission. A national funding scheme worth approximately USD 15 billion overall, and a brainchild of BJP Prime Minister Narendra Modi, the Smart Cities Mission had the goal to turn 100 Indian cities into 'digital and sustainable cities'. Criticising smart city projects as environmentally unsustainable and unequal, Banerjee promised to build a 'green', more equitable city instead. This stark decision was partially revised later, as the West Bengal Government compromised to build a 'green smart' city, a syncretism which in fact retains the same structure and components of the proposal originally developed for the Smart Cities Mission. Banerjee had opposed two key requirements of the Smart Cities Mission in particular. First, she rejected the planning criteria of Area Based Development, whereby smart infrastructures would be implemented only in selected areas of the city, arguing that would enhance urban inequality. Second, Banerjee criticised the creation of a separate administrative entity, named Special Purpose Vehicle, for managing the projects, as undemocratic. Funnily enough, the 'green smart city' that is now under construction features several Area Based Development projects and is managed by the New Town Green Smart City Corporation Limited, which is… a Special Purpose Vehicle.

© The Author(s), under exclusive license to Springer Nature Switzerland AG 2025
I. Antenucci, *Future-proofed*,
https://doi.org/10.1007/978-3-031-86429-2_2

27

28   I. ANTENUCCI

Smart, green, or both, the future city that has been promised and planned appears a remote fantasy, as New Town continues to battle with poor planning and rife inequality. And yet, albeit whimsical and uncertain in its concrete prospects (or precisely because of that?), the smart city project immediately proved to be very effective in mobilising socioeconomic forces and initiatives, from real estate operations to city policies, residents' aspirations, and activism. This chapter charts how narratives of smart futures in New Town Kolkata and Cape Town have become engines that drive processes of urban transformation in the present. By narratives, here I refer to a heterogenous collation of projects and plans, individual views, and institutional storylines, which concur in framing imaginaries of urban futures at the intersection of technologies, finance, policies, and forms of life. In looking at such constructs, I tap into a body of scholarship crossing over Science and Technology Studies (STS) and urban studies, which has in recent years drawn attention to the ways in which socio-technical imaginaries (Jasanoff, 2015) are at once 'descriptive of potential futures and prescriptive about the futures that ought to be pursued', (Miller, 2020, p. 367) thus shaping city politics, economies, and cultural practices.[1] For Sadowski and Bendor (2019), for example, the smart city imaginary promoted by companies like IBM and Cisco not only serves their commercial strategies, but plots an urban future that reinforces existing socio-political orders. More in general, Andrew Karvonen notes that urban imaginaries 'involve the strategic construction and promotion of a coherent set of ideals that bring the future into the present and catalyze urban stakeholders to focus their collective energies on a shared agenda of change' (2020, p. 420). Such constructs need to be critically unpacked to expose the values and assumptions underpinning them, and how those might be configuring uneven social landscapes. Building upon these insights, I argue that narratives and imaginaries of

---

[1] See, among others: Sepehr, P., & Felt, U. (2023). Urban Imaginaries as Tacit Governing Devices: The Case of Smart City Vienna. *Science, Technology, & Human Values.* https://doi.org/10.1177/01622439231178597; Karvonen, A. (2020) Urban Techno-Politics: Knowing, Governing, and Imagining the City. *Science as Culture.* https://doi.org/10.1080/09505431.2020.1766011; Miller, T. R. (2020). Imaginaries of Sustainability: The Techno-politics of Smart Cities. *Science as Culture* 29 (3): 365–87, 367; Sadowski, J., & Bendor, R. (2019). Selling Smartness: Corporate Narratives and the Smart City as a Sociotechnical Imaginary. *Science, Technology, & Human Values,* 44(3), 540–563. https://doi.org/10.1177/0162243918806061

smartness in New Town Kolkata and Cape Town have operated performatively in generating effects, which are predicated upon visions of the future, but are, at the same time, making those futures happen. This nexus between description and prescription, imagination and production, anticipation and action, is precisely the stuff of speculation. On these grounds then, I propose a notion of speculative urbanism that is 'broader than finance', in that it captures the multiple ways—political, governmental, and cultural—in which visions of the future are productively folded into the remaking of the present.

This chapter starts by briefly reviewing the histories of smart city projects in New Town Kolkata and Cape Town. In so doing, I stress the huge socio-spatial contradictions that persist in both cities, against which the smart city remains an ambiguous, contradictory, and elusive vision. But I also draw attention to the socio-economic and political ferment that the narratives of the future city have sparked. I then examine more specifically two projects associated with the smart city: the Bengal Silicon Valley—a massive development for accommodating tech companies—in New Town Kolkata, and the Silicon Cape—an ecosystem for tech startups—in Cape Town. Despite their differences, both are projects of tech-clustering with remarkable impacts on urban environments, demonstrating how narratives of future smartness have shaped ongoing urban transformations. Wrapping up insights from these case studies, I conclude the chapter by formulating an expanded and polysemic notion of speculative urbanism.

THE GHOST CITY GOES SMART

In New Town Kolkata, the 'green smart city' is only the latest chapter of three decades of dysfunctional urbanisation.[2] The site was planned in the early nineties as a township, and a Special Economic Zone (SEZ) for the IT industry, in the rural area of Rajarhat, on the eastern fringes of Kolkata. The Left Front government, then in power in West Bengal, resorted to a nineteenth-century colonial law to expropriate lands from farmers and villagers. Protests were met with police brutality. Thousands were jailed, some were killed. In the following years, corporate enclaves, gated communities, and luxury shopping malls began to appear amidst

---

[2] For a detailed account of the history of New Town see Dey et al. (2013), *Beyond Kolkata: Rajarhat and the Dystopia of Urban Imagination* (Routledge India).

wastelands and rural villages. With no more lands or livelihoods, many of the Rajarhat inhabitants had no option but toiling in the fringes of the new urban economy, as street vendors, domestic workers, or suppliers of raw materials for construction sites. Migrant construction workers, mostly from other areas of West Bengal, also moved to New Town to build the new high-raises, often living in makeshift settlements near their workplace. In parallel, the low cost of labour and land attracted IT firms, such as IBM, Tata Consultancy Services, Wipro, and Accenture. But far from turning New Town into a cluster of innovation and leadership, these company branches run the more basic and menial tasks of the industry, such as software beta testing and business process outsourcing (Rossiter, 2016). A few private universities and hospitals, the occasional museum, and some leisure facilities followed. Yet the township never evolved into the global corporate hub—'the new Singapore'—that was planned and promised. Heavily financialised, the development of New Town severely suffered from the global crisis of 2008. Much of the construction stopped, leaving behind a paradoxical landscape of unfinished infrastructures, unsold houses, highly securitised enclaves, slums, and stray cattle. In 2011, Ananya Roy described the township as 'the ghost town of home-grown neoliberalism, one where the ruins of the suburban middle-class dream are starkly visible' (Roy, 2011, 275). When the BJP administration launched the Smart Cities Mission, in 2015, New Town was stuck in a dystopian condition (Dey et al., 2013). The funding scheme presented local authorities with a unique opportunity to rescue the township from failure and decay.

The Smart City Proposal (SCP) for New Town was the result of negotiations among several public agencies, consultants, and corporate stakeholders, including the New Town Kolkata Development Authority, the Housing Infrastructure Development Corporation of West Bengal (HIDCO), Future Cities Catapult, Cisco, the American Chamber of Commerce in India, the Confederation of Indian Industry, and the National Association of Software and Service Companies. The requirements of the Smart Cities Mission prescribed indeed to form partnerships with the corporate sector in the planning process. As reported in the proposal document, the overall cost of the project in New Town (Rs 1532.41 Crores, approximately USD 304.6 million) was partially covered by public funding and partially reliant on public–private partnerships. In order to make the project sustainable, New Town Kolkata Development Authority planned to levy GIS-based property taxes and to raise the cost of building plan and occupancy fees for the plots of land that are still available for development. Core of the proposal was the Pan City Solution, a holistic system of digital infrastructures and centralised urban management (Smart City proposal, 2015). Yet the document is somewhat inconsistent. Part of it lists technologies that tick all the boxes of smart city standards: sensors, trackers, and cameras everywhere—on bus shelters, waste bins, water meters, light poles, etc.; mobile apps delivering all sorts of services; a single command and control room—the big 'urban brain'—integrating and processing all the data coming from city-wide sensors. At the same time, the proposal is concerned with the most basic urban infrastructures, such as roads and sidewalks, public toilets, sewerage, and street lights. This might seem odd. One would assume that a smart city is only planned when all the essential infrastructures are already in place. Instead, the proposal for New Town seeks at once to plan for advanced digital technologies, and to fix the lack of basic urban facilities, absent which the smart city could hardly ever take shape. Overall, these plans look like a unique hybrid where different temporalities and technopolitical agendas uneasily sit together. As Ayona Datta writes about Dholera, the first Indian smart city, planned in the home state of Prime Minister Modi, Gujarat, 'provincialising' smart cities in India means attending to the ways in which local, postcolonial histories shape narratives and urban development (Datta, 2015, p.9). In the case of New Town, this means redeeming the township from two decades of planning failures, and from a 'ghost city' reputation. The goal to accelerate urban and economic development through digital infrastructures must coexist with a need to provide essential infrastructures and services. At the same time, as Datta argues, building on the work of historian Ravi Kalia, smart cities must be positioned in India's postcolonial project of modernisation through utopian urbanism and the creation of new towns such as Chandigarh, Bhubaneswar, and Gandhinagar (Datta, 2015, drawing on Kalia, 1990, 1997, 2004). In his research, Kalia demonstrates how the making of new capital cities became a vehicle for building post-independence national identity and for affirming specific visions of government and society. This process continues today with smart city programmes, through which the Modi administration seeks to materialise its neoliberal-nationalist agenda through urban (re)making. At the same time, Banerjee's opposition and alternative 'green smart' city project also project a distinct political programme—populist and pro-poor, West Bengal-focused but with national aspirations. As they hit the ground at the urban scale, as in New Town, smart city projects bring together a range of different actors, both institutional and non, through relationships of cooperation, competition, and conflict. In the case of New Town, these actors include government bodies such as the New Town Kolkata Development Authority, state agencies like HIDCO and WEBEL, several consultancy firms, and a huge number of contractors. And it is through the relationships between such actors that specific political agendas are implemented, or attempted at least, as forms of urbanism.

Seen from this angle, smart city projects appear as privileged sites of *urban statecraft*—how the state is 'configured and given effect' through the making and governance of urban infrastructures (Cirolia & Harber, 2022, p. 2444). Forged in the context of African urban studies, the concept of urban statecraft is nevertheless apt to capture 'multi-scalar processes' well beyond the region, as it 'reflects (and is at the same time shaped by) complex webs of intergovernmental relations, transnational flows and local practices that shape cities and the lives of their residents' (Cirolia & Harber, 2022, p. 2433). Although the scope of this chapter is not to assess how the state is assembled and works at the urban scale, the lens of urban statecraft is very helpful to make sense of the forms of urbanism that smart city projects materialise. Later in this chapter, we will take a closer look at examples of these processes across specific projects. For now, let us dwell some more on New Town, where the smart city has resulted in a paradoxical and suspended urbanisation. While the city remains deprived of critical utilities and services, the few smart buildings and infrastructures that have been completed are surrounded by vacant lots and building sites. Yet this suspended condition is far from hollow. On the contrary, it is teeming with activities, investments, and expectations. Even though the smart city that appeared on master plans and advertising material seemed a world apart from the reality of New Town, it has been nevertheless driving and shaping economic initiatives as well as urban governance.

A conversation with JS, a bureaucrat with first-hand knowledge of urban processes, was particularly enlightening on the generative power that the smart city narrative exerted on both the economic and governmental grounds. Over a two decades career in different municipal bodies and parastatal agencies in Kolkata, JS has amassed a wealth of insights on New Town's urban development: he claims to 'know everything that needs to be known' about the township. Albeit not a supporter of Prime Minister Modi, JS was enthusiast about the smart city project since day one, and firmly believed it was a great opportunity for New Town. He claims that until then, the township had been failing 'because there was no strategy, no vision for the future. The smart city is a vision of the future. That is what matters more.. seeing, knowing what kind of city we want to build' (Interview 1, 2015). JS is very much aware of the political stakes around the smart city, particularly those placed by the BJP government: in his words, the 100 Smart Cities are 'Modi's global business card', something to show off as proof of economic power and attractiveness. He is also conscious of the many flaws of the smart city projects, particularly of the ways in which they fail to address structural problems of urban poverty. Nevertheless, JS sees the potential of the smart city in that 'a vision (*of the future*, a/n) means hope, means purpose, means that we know where we are going': and this is very effective in attracting investors. He explains how the news of inclusion in the smart city scheme had immediately tangible effects, in that investors (especially in the real estate sector) were reassured that money was on its way to New Town again, and so were the banks behind them (Interview 1, 2015).

The vision, seeing the future, are immediate reminders of speculation. The etymology of the word is indeed in the Latin *speculum* (mirror), *specere,* and *speculari*, which mean to observe, to examine. For a long time, before it became almost indissociable from its financial meaning, speculation primarily defined a theoretical production of knowledge. Knowledge and visualisation of the future are critical to the formation of the smart city narratives: smart city projects display a future city that will be efficient, clean, sustainable, pleasant, and wealthy. A number of different tools, media, and practices concur in assembling storylines and imaginaries around smart cities. Political discourses and conferences, advertising material from brochures to videos on social media, masterplans and renderings, seminars and workshops, polls and public consultations, are only some of them. Smart city narratives might differ even substantially, ranging from economic growth and entrepreneurial innovation to environmentalism, from social justice to transparency and accountability, and more. In the case of New Town, the storyline championed by the Smart City Mission, which revolved around tropes of technological acceleration, efficiency, and business growth, was primarily challenged by the West Bengal's Prime Minister Mamata Banerjee, who proposed a 'green smart city', with more emphasis on environmental and social measures. Yet, underneath the clamour and change of keywords, the backbone of the smart city narrative remained unchanged: attracting capital, and improving governance and quality of life through digital technologies.

Most importantly, however, narrative speculations are performative, in that they inspire, frame, and sustain, initiatives that already materialise the smart city to come. This is exactly the point made by JS, who emphasises time and again how the mere announcement that New Town was applying for the smart city funding, in 2015, was enough to revitalise the agonising business scene of the township, particularly the real estate market. 'In 2015, they were all gone' tells JS: investors, realtors, and developers were only trying to survive their failed investments and to get rid as quickly as possible of all the unsold. 'Then word is out that New Town is one of the 100 cities' JS narrates with emphasis, 'and the day after, the telephone starts ringing again all day, and you see them all (*the property developers and investors, A/N*) around town again, and also new people.. and suddenly they all ask for meetings again, they all want the land again' (Interview 2, 2017). As we speak, JS runs through his own notes and documents, where he has lists of companies and businesspeople who are currently negotiating investments in New Town. He reads aloud figures and business ideas to demonstrate how the smart city is revitalising the local economy. As I listen to JS, I get the impression that he is somehow trying to translate the smart city 'vision' into economic indicators, and to quantify the impact of the urban future on the present, as to legitimise his enthusiasm in the project with 'objective' data. But ferment in the real estate and commercial fields are not the only examples of the smart city effect. Right after the first smart city announcement, between 2015 and 2016, the New Town Kolkata Development Authority organised a series of 'citizens engagement activities', in partnership with consultancy firms such as Future Cities Catapult and Deloitte. As Gosh and Arora (2021) document, citizens' engagement around smart city planning was however largely framed by the New Town Kolkata Development Authority agenda, and organised in modalities that encouraged middle-class participation, while marginalising the input of lower-income citizens. One of my interlocutors in New Town was MB, at the time a recent graduate working for one of the consultancy firms, thus closely involved in the preparation and running of these activities, including public consultations and polls as well as workshops. In her view, the main point of the engagement activities was not so much to engage citizens in the smart city planning, but rather to start preparing them for a new form of urbanity: 'There is no smart city without smart citizens, and there was a lot of work to do in that respect in New Town. Citizens needed to learn to see themselves as smart, to think smart, to behave smart' (Interview 3, 2017). By 'smart', MB means not only familiar and comfortable with digital technologies. She referred indeed to a broader mindset and moral universe, which involved being curious about innovations, sensitive to environmental sustainability, and caring for each other and the city. Educating citizens to a smart mindset and morality was the main piece of advice that, as consultants, MB and her senior colleagues gave to the New Town Kolkata Development Authority. Yet, for MB, the duration and format of the activities planned by the New Town Kolkata Development Authority—only a few meetings, very rigid in their structure, not carefully designed in their content—was largely insufficient to this end. But at least, MB explains, the meetings brought together a bunch of like-minded residents, who understood the importance of building a new mindset and a new sense of community for the city in the making. Made up of mixed ages and gender, highly educated and mostly middle-class citizens, this group spontaneously mobilised to promote 'smart citizenship' activities among New Town residents. Between 2016 and 2018, these activities were largely coordinated and advertised through a Facebook page (now defunct). Ranging from seminars on digital technologies to meetings with 'experts', from exhibitions to family gatherings, the group's activities had the explicit mission of raising awareness among fellow citizens on what it meant to build, and live in, a smart city. In the words of PK, a female software engineer in her forties and one of the leaders of the group, 'We have a great opportunity with the government funding et cetera but if we want the city to really be smart, we as citizens need to step in.. we need to create new habits, not just tech skills but a new approach to the city.. we need citizens who are responsible, who are dynamic, who take good care of the city. That is what makes a city really smart' (Interview 4, 2016). Later in this chapter and in the followings, we will see how these ideas of smart citizenship are linked to a tradition of middle-class activism in Indian cities, which easily slip into forms of criminalisation and discrimination of other urban communities, such as street vendors. For now, however, it is important to stress how these (self) educational practices among citizens signal another path through which projections of the future city are shaping new forms of being in the actual city.

For JS, the smart city was really a 'new start' for New Town. Whether this 'new start' will eventually lead to the prosperous and sustainable urban development that has been promised is at present hard to say. What

36   I. ANTENUCCI

is nevertheless unmistakable is that a process of transformation has been put in motion by the enunciation and narratives of the city to come. In other words, the smart city projects are changing New Town already, even if there is no guarantee that the future city will ever resemble the plans.

Africa's Smartest City

'Is Cape Town a smart city? That really depends on what you mean by smart' says ZS with a smile and a glimpse of irony, shrugging her shoulders (Interview 5, 2015). On a sunny late-spring morning, in November 2015, we are sitting outside the Watershed, a former warehouse now hosting co-working spaces, a designers market, and a startup incubator. Renovated in a tasteful post-industrial style, the Watershed has timber beams ceilings, huge glass windows overlooking the beautiful harbour, and sun-filled rooms decorated with minimal, yet colourful elements. We are in the heart of the Victoria & Albert Waterfront, commonly known as the V&A: a massive reconversion of the old harbour into shopping malls, hotels and restaurants, office and residential space, and one of the flagship destinations of Cape Town's city centre. Around us, heritage sailing ships swing lazily in the harbour canals, while tourists stroll between shops and cafes. Security guards and cameras are everywhere, making sure that homeless and beggars won't spoil the fun for customers. ZS, my interlocutor, is a journalist and tech consultant in her late thirties, who has worked for both the public and private sectors. I met her at Workshop 17, a co-working space located inside the Watershed, which is a popular business venue for tech startups. ZS works for the business incubator hosted at the Watershed, which helps startups acquire the new skills they need, connect with each other and, most importantly, with investors. Previously she also advised the City of Cape Town on projects related to the planning and implementation of IT infrastructures. Because of her professional experience, ZS has an insightful perspective on smart city projects in Cape Town. More than that, in many ways ZS is a piece of the smart city herself, in that she embodies all the values and aesthetics that smart city narratives promote: young, tech-savvy, entrepreneurial-minded but sensitive to social and environmental issues, and a believer in a future of innovation and growth. For her, 'smart city' is a very ambiguous word, meaning different things to different people. 'To some people' says ZS 'smart city simply means lots of IT, lots of people using smartphones and apps and stuff, lots of IT graduates.. for other people, smart city means that life is easier, it means that things really work, that what you need in your daily life is accessible. Or that resources are managed more effectively, in a more sustainable way.. And for others, smart city means business in the first place, startups and investors and new markets. But maybe for some people it means nothing at all.. you know, if they're not part of.. lots of people in Cape Town have other priorities, food, shelter, you know' (Interview 5, 2015).

The words of ZS shed light on two key aspects of the Cape Town smart city. One is the inherent ambiguity of the overall project, which merges an at least formal commitment towards social inclusion and justice with neoliberal methods and targets; and which sees different actors— the city, the Western Cape government, parastatal agencies, the business community, and NGOs—allied in pursuing the smart city agenda. The other aspect is the deep inequality that still divides the city along racial lines. As a technopolitical project, the smart city materialises the ambivalence of post-apartheid politics at the scale of the urban state. Since the free elections of 1994, a firm commitment towards development and poverty relief has been key to South African governments, reflected in major policy frameworks such as the Reconstruction and Development Programme (RDP) and the Black Economic Empowerment (BEE). Such developmental approach remained at the core of state initiative even after the neoliberal turn of the GEAR (Growth, Employment, and Redistribution) plan, in 1996: the two strategies have been somehow cohabiting national politics for nearly three decades. This uneasy coexistence is particularly visible at the urban level, where substantial pro-poor policies, including housing and the provision of free basic services, have been juxtaposed with the growing privatisation and entrepreneurialisation of urban spaces and infrastructures. Cape Town is an old city with a complicated past: under the apartheid regime, its urban geography was aggressively rearranged to enforce racial segregation. While the central and seaside suburbs—nestled between the ocean and Table Mountain— became 'whites-only' areas, the black and coloured population was largely deported into overcrowded, underserviced townships in the Cape Flats on the south-eastern fringes of the city. Almost thirty years after the end of apartheid, Cape Town is one of the economic engines of the African continent, contributing 9.8% of South Africa's GDP, yet the socioeconomic and infrastructural gaps between the townships and the former whites-only parts of the city remain huge. Cape Town regularly features among one the most unequal cities in the world although, as Parnell and

Robinson note, it is much less unequal than a few decades ago, thanks to the anti-poverty strategies undertaken by the local government after 1994 (2012). Launched in 2000 by the city government, the Smart City Strategy explicitly aimed at overcoming the urban legacy of apartheid through IT access and literacy. The first stage of the strategy was the Smart Cape Access project, implemented between 2002 and 2007, in partnership with IT companies, Xerox and CableCom Ltd, to provide free computers and internet access to public libraries in disadvantaged areas. In 2009, the city began rolling out broadband fibre networks throughout the metropolitan area and building a platform for e-governance, with an estimated investment of R 1.7. billion (approximately USD 1.3 billion). In parallel, over the past two decades the city has seen remarkable growth in the software design and development sector. Global success stories testify to that, such as Mark Shuttleworth's company, Thwate and the Ubuntu Project; Mxit, a very popular messaging app between 2005 and 2016; and Fundamo, the world's largest provider of mobile financial services, among others (PWC, Wesgro & City of Cape Town 2013). In the wake of this trend, the creation of an 'ecosystem' for tech startups has been identified as a key growth driver for Cape Town's development, and has become the *other* focus of the smart city agenda, forcefully pursued by a network of private and public actors through a wide range of initiatives. For example, the University of Stellenbosch and the University of Cape Town have partnered with corporate funders, such as Napers and Siemens, to set up research labs in new technologies; and a number of business accelerators and incubators have been created with the task of connecting emerging companies with local global investors. As of 2021, Cape Town was home to almost 60% of tech startups in Africa (Startup Genome, 2021) and to 53% of venture capital deals in South Africa, most of which are directed precisely to tech, and especially fintech, startups (Pollio & Cirolia, 2022; SAVCA, 2017). In recent years, Cape Town has also become a major node for cloud computing on the African continent. Elastic Compute Cloud (EC2), the backbone of Amazon Web Services (AWS), the leader in the cloud computing market, was born from an Amazon development centre operating in Cape Town between 2004 and 2006. Since 2018, both AWS and Azul (Microsoft's cloud service) have opened cloud data centres in Cape Town. Furthermore, by leveraging the implementation of publicly owned fibre networks and data centres, the municipality of Cape Town has become an operator of cloud services itself. For any firm operating with data and cloud services, the presence of data centres in Cape Town offers an unquestionable logistical advantage,[3] which contributes to making the city attractive for startups as well as established companies.

Over the past decade and more, both corporate and government discourses have been framing the IT sector not only as a priority for economic growth but also as a major factor for urban transformation. *Digital Gateway to Africa*, a report compiled by consultancy firm PWC, Wesgro[4], and the City of Cape Town (2013), is very explicit in stating that Cape Town needs to become a global tech hub, or, in their words, the African Silicon Valley. The report suggests that tech companies need a smart city to expand their markets and to attract investors and skilled workforce. But despite its thriving service and tech sectors, racialised inequality is still strong, with 43,9% black households living in poverty as of 2020 (State of Cape Town Report, 2022). The spatial distribution of infrastructures, digital and non, is similarly uneven. Since the mid-1990s, a significant portion of service management, from public safety to cleaning and maintenance, has been taken up by City Improvements Districts (CIDs)—public–private partnerships funded through additional property taxes in a specific area (Didier et al., 2012). As a result, levels of digital access and the integration of services differ remarkably between suburbs, depending on the socio-economic conditions of residents. For example, the Central Business District, managed by the Central City Improvement District, is populated with objects such as 'smart benches' equipped with Wi-Fi hotspots, USB chargers, and solar panels. In 2018, four blocks of the Central Business District were designated a 'smart zone' for hosting the Connect Pilot Project, which delivered open-access fibre optic broadband to all the buildings in the block. The 'smart zone' served as 'a confined urban living laboratory for the City to design and test smart device solutions such as traffic light systems, water and electricity meter management systems, CCTV camera and Wi-Fi/Radio technology systems' ('Cape Town CBD gets smart', 2018). Other central neighbourhoods, such as De Waterkant, Green Point, Sea Point, Gardens, and Woodstock, are also heavily digitalised. Here, much of everyday life, from

---

[3] While data can be stored and processed in any location, physical proximity to the servers and computers minimises the latency of data, improving the performances and competitiveness of cloud-based applications.

[4] The official tourism, trade, and investment promotion agency for Cape Town and the Western Cape

car rides to meals and grocery delivery, from domestic work on demand to cashless payments, smoothly run on smartphones. The conditions of digital infrastructure are dramatically different in the townships, where even access to basic utilities, such as pipe water or sewerage, is historically a terrain of conflict in post-apartheid South Africa (von Schnitzler, 2016). In Khayelitsha and Mitchell's Plain, with populations of 391,749 and 310,485, respectively, broadband coverage is scarce and residents are forced to access the Internet via mobile devices, which is the most expensive way (State of Cape Town Report, 2022). In 2016, the #DataMustFall campaign exposed how low-income South Africans were largely locked out from the digital economy (Cameron, 2017). Starting as a Twitter hashtag, the movement quickly grew to a mass protest against the unaffordable prices of mobile data and the oligopolistic conditions of the market. For around 50% of South Africans, one GB of mobile data costed them between 15 and 40% of their income. Residents were often offline in neighbourhoods where public Wi-Fi was not available.

Smart city plans and rhetoric notwithstanding, the geography of digitalisation in Cape Town still disturbingly reflects the spatial organisation of the apartheid city. Amidst these contradictions, the smart city appears as a process of urban statecraft in which different rationalities converge, appealing to disparate and even conflicting interests. Despite its tangible social shortcomings, the narrative of the smart city as a vehicle towards a better urban future remains a powerful driver of initiatives and transformation. PDW, a former city manager who worked closely with business accelerators on the smart city agenda, makes that very clear in the reflections he shares with me. For PDW, the smart city is in the first place an idea and 'a *vision* of the city we want to live in in ten years, twenty years.. that inspires the things we do now, to make it possible to actually live in that city, to build that city' (Interview 6, 2016). It is significant that the same word, *vision*, had come up as well in the words of a former city official of New Town Kolkata, to describe a process that mobilises the future to manage and transform the present. In PDW's view, making a smart city means, first and foremost, creating a favourable environment for innovation and business, and that is achieved by attracting the best talents and by giving them support, opportunities, and 'good reasons to stay'. These 'leaders' in their sector will then attract other talents, and that's how you create a hub. 'It's happening already', PDW goes on 'Go to the Waterfront, go to Woodstock, you can see those people, you can feel the energy. The city has changed a lot already and will keep changing.. for the better'.

When I ask how these changes are impacting upon poorer communities, and fulfilling the missions of inclusion and social justice stated in the Smart City Strategy, he replies that those are huge problems that cannot be fixed overnight. Reiterating the well-consumed neoliberal liturgy of trickle-down, PDW argues that 'Yes we all want to fight poverty, but how do you really fight poverty? I say you don't do that by giving free internet to everybody. You do that by creating growth'. He predicts that digital infrastructures, new companies, and technological innovations will create more jobs, better salaries, and entrepreneurial opportunities, from which everyone will benefit.

As we have seen so far, the urban histories and present conditions of New Town Kolkata and Cape Town are profoundly different. Yet one thing is strikingly similar: how smart city discourses, declined according to the specificities of the context, work as productive frameworks for urban transformation regardless of their unlikeliness, distance from everyday problems, and failure to address severe urban issues. To better illustrate this argument, the remainder of this chapter will zoom in on two projects of urban tech-clustering: the Bengal Silicon Valley in New Town Kolkata, and the Silicon Cape in Cape Town.

TECH CHIMERAS AND URBAN TRANSFORMATION

The Bengal Silicon Valley

Shortly after withdrawing New Town from the Smart Cities Mission, and launching the 'green smart city' as an alternative, in 2017, West Bengal's chief minister Mamata Banerjee announced a colossal new project: the Bengal Silicon Valley. A 200 acres land plot stretching along Biswa Bangla Sarani, New Town's main arterial road, the Bengal Silicon Valley is presented as a 'futuristic hub that will catalyze the IT ecosystem in the state'[5]. The project is managed by the West Bengal Housing Infrastructure Development Corporation, commonly known as HIDCO, the government agency that is officially 'trying to develop Rajarhat, New Town as a futuristic smart city'[6]. HIDCO has been in charge of the land allotment process, through which companies have applied for, and purchased if successful, the available plots).

[5] https://bengalsiliconvalley.in/
[6] https://www.wbhidcoltd.com/aboutus

In the official promotional video of the Bengal Silicon Valley, released in 2018[7] by Webel, aerial shots show steel and glass buildings sitting on a green, lush landscape. Autonomous vehicles roaming around the manicured gardens under the watch of AI-enabled cameras, sun-filled workspaces, and long lines of flashing server racks: the video is a carousel of Silicon Valley tropes, strikingly at odds with the actual appearance of the site. Paused during the Covid-19 pandemic, still in December 2023 the 200 acres of the IT hub are indeed only a huge construction site, where most buildings are in the very early stages of construction (West Bengal with Rohit, 2023a, 2023b). Looking at the foundations' pits and at the concrete frameworks, the official 'opening for business' date of 2025 feels unlikely at best. Yet in the meantime the project is already performing its designated function of catalyser for investments, in the IT sector and beyond. Since 2018, the media has regularly announced new rounds of applications for land allotment from leading IT firms, both homegrown and foreign. News on the competition among famous companies for securing land plots, as well as detailing the ever-growing amounts of money invested into the project has contributed to assembling a storyline of success in the making for the township. As the list of investors grew longer, so did the size of the development, which went from the initial 100 acres of land, to 200 acres, to potentially 250 as proposed in 2022 (Tnn, 2018; Chakraborti, 2022a). The project is Mamata Banerjee's own political speculation, which she pitched against the central government plans in order to strengthen her leadership in West Bengal. Amidst a poverty-relief-oriented agenda, featuring several programmes of cash transfer schemes for the poorest, the Bengal Silicon Valley project stands out as a strategy to captivate big capital and cultivate West Bengal's global positioning. In contrast with BJP's aggressive neoliberalism, the Bengal Silicon Valley marks the Trinamool Congress's own pathway to promote economic growth, technological innovation, and national prestige. In line with Banerjee's highly personalised style of leadership (Ray Chaudhuri, 2022) in public discourse the IT hub is closely associated to their persona. For example, the promo video begins by presenting the project as 'inspired by the Honorable Chief Minister of West Bengal', and ends with a picture of a smiling Mamata. In other advertising material published by HIDCO, the storyline of the

---

[7] https://www.youtube.com/watch?v=QtNKZ1JrgOc&t=47s

Bengal Silicon Valley as a vessel for regional growth is packaged with details of prospective tenants, statistics on West Bengal's digital economy, and popular slogans like 'Data is new oil[8]'. The brochure ends with a Namaste-greeting Mamata, a robot head, and the invitation to 'Live the Silicon Dream'.

As a mega infrastructure project, the Bengal Silicon Valley appears as a bet and as a test for Banerjee's and the Trinamool Congress's agenda, and is promoted through narratives that explicitly speculate on the future city—living the dream, and making it real—to attract investors and fulfil the political promises made. Agencies, such as HIDCO and Webel, are actively enrolled not only in the technical management of the project, but also in propagating such narratives. Here, statecraft operates through the production of speculative imaginaries of the city, which connect institutional actors to the private sector.

Indeed, with land plots in the Bengal Silicon Valley filling up with prestigious buyers, the real estate sector has been quick to react. According to Indian real estate platform Proptiger, there are currently 832 real estate projects in New Town, of which 474 are ready to move in, 298 are under construction, 35 are new launches, and 10 are launching soon. Market analyses describe New Town as a prime location for real estate in Kolkata, where prices have gone up by 52% over the past 4/5 years (Property in New Town Kolkata, n.d.). Many of these new properties are upscale and hi-tech gated communities, featuring rooftop swimming pools, lush gardens, and all sorts of amenities, designed to accommodate the new corporate elite drawn by the Bengal Silicon Valley. MN, a Kolkata-based real estate market analyst, observes that the Bengal Silicon Valley has been the real game-changer for the development of New Town, what revitalised investments and the real estate market in the area. In her views, the smart city was already 'a big move, something that put the place in the spotlight (…) but the Bengal Silicon Valley gave us numbers to work with: buildings, offices, number of workers expected.. developers and realtors and investors can work with that, can plan on that.. they will know how many people are moving here, what kind of jobs they have, salaries, lifestyle.. so they can propose solutions that suit those new people'. MN's remarks capture how powerfully the Bengal Silicon Valley project, albeit little more than on paper, is already changing the urban fabric. As she notes, 'the

---

[8] https://bengalsiliconvalley.in/assets/brouchure/silicon_valley_slide.pdf

smart city, the Bengal Silicon Valley, make the place desirable for people to work and live here.. because they see a certain lifestyle.. innovation, smart city, educated people' (Interview 7, 2018). For MN, this generates a virtuous circle, whereby properties and facilities are built that are attractive to 'that kind of people', who will then buy and move to New Town, thus creating 'that kind of lifestyle' that will make the city more attractive to other like-minded people, and so more buyers will follow, 'and so on, that's how it works with real estate' (Interview 7, 2018). MN'S account of New Town's property market points to an entanglement of narratives, aspirations, and investments, that is crucial to the development of the township, even beyond real estate. Long before opening for business, the Bengal Silicon Valley is already reconfiguring the city by increasing asset value, and therefore shaping the socio-economic composition of local residents. In spite of Banerjee's pro-poor commitment, her flagship project is in fact contributing to the deepening of urban polarisation in New Town, drawing in more upper middle-class households at the expense of lower-income dwellers.

The pursuit of a certain type of urban aesthetics, which suit certain standards and desires—those of affluent residents, but also those commonly associated with urban modernity and development—is also reflected in the bylaws proposed to make the area around the Bengal Silicon Valley a hawkers-free zone (Chakraborti, 2022b). Not dissimilarly from many Indian cities, the presence of hawkers (informal street vendors) on pavements has long been a field of tension and negotiation in New Town[9]. Over the past few years, the New Town Kolkata Development Authority has made repeated, and mostly unsuccessful, attempts to clear hawkers from sidewalks and relocate them to planned market areas. Yet makeshift shacks and stalls keep returning to 'encroach' public roads and walkways, causing complaints among residents. In the next chapter, we will see how the presence of informal vendors is framed by New Town's authority as a security issue, becoming the terrain in which new surveillance technologies are tested. For now, however, it is important to note how the removal of hawkers from the streets is driven by visions of the future city—digital, clean, worldly, and wealthy—as well as part of its making. The conversations I had with three members of a Facebook group of New Town residents gave me many insights into

---

[9] For accounts on hawkers and the informal sector in Indian urban politics see, among others: Chatterjee (2006); Mahadevan and Naqvi (2017); Rao (2013) and Roy (2009).

the expectations and concerns of middle-class dwellers around smart city projects and urban governance. Explicitly banning political and religious debates, the group presents itself as a 'community for like-minded individuals' to discuss 'new developments, new stores, new places to see...' and more generally, anything that is happening in the township. Albeit public and open to everyone, the group has a clear middle-class connotation, with a large number of posts asking for information on private schools, searching for domestic help, reviewing restaurants, and discussing memberships at local business clubs. The group also frequently features complaints about the presence of hawkers on the streets, with members lamenting the lack of hygiene and space for pedestrians, and calling for local authorities to intervene. My three contacts from the Facebook group all emphasise how the presence of street vendors is a major issue for the liveability of New Town, and for its development into a smart city. For AC, a group member in her late thirties who identifies as an accountant and mother of three, hawkers can only have a place in New Town 'if they follow the rules like everyone else, and only occupy the spaces that have been assigned to them, rather than public spaces that are for everyone'. AC believes that in a modern, civilised city, like New Town wants to be, 'you can't have the *stain* of people encroaching everywhere, making walking unsafe and dirt and noise'. (Personal Conversation 1, 2018). AG, a professional in his fifties, argues that 'making a smart city is not only the government's project, it is in the interest of everyone so it is the responsibility of everyone. But if you want to build a smart city, you can't have roads that are obstructed and messy and dirty (*because of hawkers, a/n*).. that is ridiculous. It is everyone's responsibility to expose that and to put pressure (*on the authorities, a/n*) to have a clean and orderly city, before we have a smart city' (Personal Conversation 2, 2018). For RS, an HR manager, 'hawkers are a problem of the old town.. they shouldn't be a problem in the new town'. The reference is clearly to the old city of Kolkata, with its legacy of overcrowding, poverty, and dysfunction, to which the development of New Town was supposed to be antithetical—a point that resonates with reflections by Dey, Samaddar, and Sen in their book 'Beyond Kolkata' (2013). 'We are building the Bengal Silicon valley, but do they have hawkers in the Silicon Valley of California? If we want to attract that kind of companies, that kind of people, the city must be ready for them' (Personal Conversation 3, 2018). The comments made by these residents of New Town make clear how, as smart city imaginaries circulate among the locals, they become infused with ideas of urban order that

46   I. ANTENUCCI

reflect certain social hierarchies, either existing or desired. As they seek to produce specific urban futures, speculations on the smart city incorporate and reinforce site-specific tensions and patterns of discrimination.

The Silicon Cape

If New Town Kolkata is set to become the Bengal Silicon Valley, for over a decade Cape Town has been building the 'Silicon Cape'. Unlike the Bengal Silicon Valley, the Silicon Cape is not a physical place, but a more elusive creature: an ecosystem of tech startups and companies, universities, and investors. Conceived and shaped by a coalition of entrepreneurs, the project of turning Cape Town into a cluster—or Africa's leading cluster— for the digital industry has developed over the past fifteen years through partnerships between corporate and institutional actors, such as the City of Cape Town and the Western Cape government.

Technically, the Silicon Cape is in the first place a business incubator[10], with the mission of promoting tech entrepreneurship in the city. Founded in 2009 by South African entrepreneurs Vinny Lingham and Justin Stanford, Silicon Cape connects local startups with investors 'angels', venture capital, and the like—and institutional partners. The organisation borrows heavily from the Silicon Valley narrative of the 'ecosystem' and plays into the similarities between the San Francisco Bay Area and Cape Town—beautiful nature, great universities, and relaxed lifestyle—to articulate a discursive and aesthetic framework for their initiatives. More broadly, however, the Silicon Cape has become a popular synonymous for strategies of tech-focused urban development. The parallel between the Western Cape and the Silicon Valley is constantly reiterated across media outlets and everyday conversations, and is reinforced by examples of notable, homegrown, entrepreneurial success, such as Mark Shuttleworth, founder of Thwate and promoter of Ubuntu; Chris Pinkham, among the creators of the first internet service provider (ISP) in Cape Town and, many years later, of Elastic Compute Cloud (EC2), Amazon's cloud computing architecture; or the already mentioned Lingham and Stanford, who came back home from California, and gave life to the Silicon Cape initiative. Framing Cape Town as an ideal location for tech startups has been pivotal in laying out another smart city storyline,

---

[10] One of the most prominent among the more than 20 incubators, accelerators, and catalysts for tech business in town.

focused on entrepreneurship and individual success, alongside the city's smart city strategy. Yet, as Andrea Pollio (2020) notes, there is more than one possible genealogy of the Silicon Cape, not all of them equally popular. For Pollio, the fact that Cape Town had become a destination for business service offshoring, in the early 2000s, might be another meaningful explanation for the concentration of entrepreneurial energies and infrastructural investments in the area. Many major companies, including IBM, Shell, and Lufthansa, moved their call centres to the city, attracted by what Pollio describes as 'two important colonial legacies: the multilingualism of the Cape and the low labour cost' (2020, para. 1). The offshoring process generated 'not only a hunger for a specialised, entrepreneurial workforce but also developmental infrastructural investments, which resulted in a decently sized and relatively cheap broadband connectivity' (Pollio, 2020, p. 5). This alternative genealogy of tech-clustering in Cape Town shifts the focus from mythologies of individual success to a more comprehensive account of economic and technological processes. The fact that large companies, including tech giant IBM, moved part of their operations to Cape Town, more than two decades ago, not only stimulated an entrepreneurial culture, but also put the city on the map of global finance. Those were the socio-economic and cultural seeds for the rise of Cape Town as a major tech cluster in the African continent. Over the past two decades, Capetonian entrepreneurial circles and government bodies—the City of Cape Town and the Western Cape Government—have joined forces to set up a number of incubator and accelerator programmes for tech startups. If entrepreneurs have actively lobbied for the creation of a business-friendly environment, the City of Cape Town has devoted significant resources to the rolling out of ICT infrastructures in the urban area. They have also adopted specific policies, including business development programmes targeting young people from marginalised backgrounds, to support the growth of a tech startup ecosystem in the city. For Andrea Pollio and Liza Cirolia (2022), this alliance between corporate lobbies and municipal authorities is an example of what Rossi and Di Bella (2017) define as *startup urbanism*, that is, a set of urban policies supporting technological innovation and/or capitalist interests. In the making of the Silicon Cape, as part of Cape Town's smart city strategy, startup urbanism becomes the framework for local statecraft. And as the broader smart city strategy, the Silicon Cape is also marked by the compresence of developmentalism, with a focus on digital access and inclusion for marginalised urban communities, and a neoliberal approach, which proposes digital entrepreneurialism as a solution to poverty and racial discrimination (Pollio, 2020; Pollio & Cirolia, 2022). An example of this is the Bandwidth Barn, a tech incubator established by the Western Cape Government in partnership with the Cape Innovation & Technology Initiative (CiTi), a non-profit organisation that aims to promote digital growth in Cape Town[11]. The Barn operates a branch in the township of Khayelitsha, where it hosts several training programmes aimed at the inclusion of township youth in the digital innovations and economies, where participants can learn technical skills and access networking as well as funding opportunities. The training offered includes entrepreneurial bootcamps, hackathons, 'digital citizens' programmes, and professional mentorship. Participation is however tied to specific requirements, such as presenting an entrepreneurial project, writing a business model, or competing against others. In other words, inclusion is conditional upon subscribing to entrepreneurial values. PV, a former consultant of CiTi, explains that the Barn approach is different from previous educational initiatives in the townships because it is 'fully pragmatic, tailored to business, and *future-fit* (…)not just about teaching people skills, but helping them see their future, and the future of this city, of this country, and to find their place in it. (…)Not to act like disadvantaged people from the township, but like the successful entrepreneurs they're gonna be one day, soon. This is the main training' (Interview 8, 2016). The term 'future-fit' returns very often in Barn's own narrative, i.e. in their own their website: 'We build future societies, today'. The purpose of initiatives like the Barn is not humanitarian, but strategic towards unlocking the potential for growth, the talents, the skills among township youth. Resources are not distributed universally, but targeted to identify and support 'the excellence', i.e. future entrepreneurs that will 'make a difference' in the economy: 'This is not charity, it is an investment, and it will pay back' (Interview 8, 2016). These remarks suggest that, in the narrative and operational framework of the Silicon Cape, urban inequality has become the terrain for experimenting techniques of poverty management that combine a developmental mission with market-oriented pedagogical intervention (Ferguson, 2010, 2015; Pollio, 2019). In doing so, they also operationalise a speculative logic. In line with the

---

[11] https://uvuafrica.com/our-story/

Bottom of the Pyramid (BOP) approach, government agencies, corporate circles, and NGOs are indeed aligned in forging a new generation of entrepreneurs and digital citizens among the township youth, which are expected to raise themselves out of poverty while contributing to the growth of city's tech ecosystem. A calculated distribution of resources (infrastructures, training, funding) is deployed in order to generate innovation and value within a certain time frame. In this process, specific futures—i.e. of the individual young entrepreneur in the making, as well as of a 'smarter' township as part of a 'smarter' city—are envisioned and performed in the present through a set of educational practices.

If the Khayelitsha township is the urban frontier of the Silicon Cape and of the smart city, Woodstock is the core of the startup ecosystem. Over the past two decades, this historically working-class neighbourhood has been largely 'requalified' and redeveloped to accommodate new tenants—entrepreneurs, professionals, investors—and to suit their lifestyle, while old, low-income residents have been pushed out by rising prices and new, unfriendly neighbours (Boiles-Leonard, 2023). Only a few kilometres away from the Central Business District, Woodstock used to be home to manufacturers and workshops, as well as to communities of white, black, and coloured residents. Today, factories have been turned into business parks, co-working spaces, high-end flats, and fancy markets. KM, a white real estate agent in her late forties, has been witnessing the transformation of Woodstock first-hand since startups have begun flocking in.

Having been involved in 'dozens and dozens' of real estate operations in the area, from small unit rentals, to the redevelopment of major buildings, KM has seen demand and prices per square meter spiking up, 'even fivefold in some cases'. She has also seen the socio-economic composition of the neighbourhood change dramatically, with an incoming cohort of young and affluent customers looking for a home. From her point of view, the proliferation of startups in the area is driving a change that is entirely positive: 'The new residents care more about their properties and the neighbourhood in general, they do a lot to keep everything clean and safe, but they also take initiatives to build a healthy community for their families and their children' (Interview 9, 2016). Implicit in these remarks is a judgement of the 'old' and lower-income residents, who are portrayed, by comparison, as neglecting their houses and as conducting 'unhealthy' lifestyles. This echoes a widespread, racialised narrative that represents mostly black low-income households in central neighbourhoods as dirty, unreliable, prone to addiction, and more. Such narrative, a trope of post-apartheid white anxiety, circulated more heavily than usual as such communities were being evicted from neighbourhoods like Woodstock to make room for new real estate speculations (Boiles-Leonard, 2023). But as Boiles-Leonard documents, similar narratives, or at least part of them, keep marking tensions amidst different socio-ethnic groups in Woodstock. For KM, however, it is 'just great' that new Woodstock residents are setting 'higher standards for the neighbourhood', insofar as that fuels the property market. When I ask her what she thinks about the Silicon Cape and, more broadly, of smart city projects, KM admits that it is quite unclear to her what those are exactly about. From her professional point of view, the most interesting thing about those is, again, their impact on real estate. 'A smart city, whatever that means, is a place where people wants to live.. and the startups bring innovations, they bring interesting people, and wealth.. they are changing the city for the better, and that is good for the market'. Recent developments in Woodstock, such as tech campus Brickfield Canvas, co-working spaces like the Woodstock Hub and the Woodstock Exchange, or leisure spaces like The Old Biscuit Mill, are for KM examples and symbols of what the smart city is going to look like. 'Innovative, attractive, but treasuring the heritage at the same time.. I surely hope more of Cape Town will look like that in the future!' (Interview 9, 2016). Notably, with their security systems and selected customers, those places are also the symbols of the neighbourhood's heavy gentrification, and of the marginalisation of lower-income residents.

AG, a capetonian freelance journalist who has been following the tech sector for over a decade, observes that there is a lot of rhetoric around the idea of a Silicon Cape: 'It is clearly a brand, and a marketing strategy, to sell a certain idea of city and urban economy'. But for AG that is not a negative thing at all: on the contrary, he sees that as a powerful driver of urban change. To become a global tech hub and a smart city, AG claims, infrastructures and money matter, of course, and in that respect Cape Town has more to offer than any other South African city: 'But you also need something else... you need to sell a vision, a culture, a lifestyle. Just like the Silicon Valley is more than that (*money and infrastructures, a/n*).. it is a lifestyle, a dream. If you can sell that dream, the right people will come, and they will bring more money, and more ideas, and more success, and the city will be even more attractive, and so on.

It is a virtuous circle, and it's happening already' (Interview 10, 2016). As Andrea Pollio notes, narrating the Silicon Cape is an ontological act 'because it actively contributes to the production of the Silicon Cape as a fertile terrain for technological innovation, virtuous investment cycles, favourable legislative actions, networking opportunities and supporting urban infrastructures' (2020, 2717). These words capture quite acutely the impact of projects and narratives like the Silicon Cape and the Bengal Silicon Valley regardless of their tangible completion, if ever achievable. The Bengal Silicon Valley is an early-stage, albeit massive, construction site; and, as an ecosystem, the Silicon Cape is a shifting and elusive undertaking. It is unlikely that Cape Town will be able to compete with the Californian digital industry in the near future, or that New Town Kolkata will soon become the Asian hub for tech companies. Yet these projects work like generative frameworks, as engines for urban transformation, driving economic initiatives and imaginaries around which different urban actors align. The differences between New Town Kolkata and Cape Town are, of course, stark: a greenfield, largely state-led development the former; a polycentric process, in which smart initiatives are distributed among a number of public and private actors, the latter. Yet, while both cities keep struggling with sore inequality, narratives of the smart city to come have already colonised the present: flows of capital, policies, and socio-cultural aspirations of smartness are rearranging the urban fabric at multiple levels, from real estate prices to poverty management. As the urban future is at once not only envisaged, but *materialised* in multiple ways—by investing, training, preparing, cleaning up—the making of smart cities presents a mode of urbanism that is exquisitely speculative.

Broader than Finance

Approximately ten years after the article in which Michael Goldman (2011) first introduced the idea of speculative urbanism, a recent theme issue (Leitner & Sheppard, 2023) proposes that the notion has outgrown its original economic framings, embracing the numerous socio-cultural practices through which urban futures are anticipated and constructed. More specifically, Desiree Fields (2023) argues that research on speculative urbanism needs to move beyond the mere financial-real estate nexus, exploring the various vocabularies and temporalities through which finance connects to 'the socio-ecological, the socio-technical, and the everyday' (2023, p. 514). Inspired by this work, and drawing upon my findings in New Town Kolkata and Cape Town presented so far, here I propose a concept of speculative urbanism that is even more spacious and polysemic, encompassing forms of speculation that are not merely, or not primarily financial, but refer to multiple modalities of envisioning, anticipating, and capitalising upon the urban future.

At one level, I propose that speculative urbanism is a form of urban statecraft. The smart city projects examined in this book are eminently political speculations: high-stakes operations through which state action is legitimised at city scale. As government bodies—in closer or looser partnerships with capitalist agents—propose visions of the future city, they also operationalise those futures as tools for urban governance and transformation in the present. In New Town Kolkata, we have seen how plans for urban infrastructures become the battlefield where different components of the Indian state—the federal government and the West Bengal government—compete over alternative visions of development, distribution of resources, and management of power. At the same time, we have seen how the making of a smart city, and especially the Bengal Silicon Valley, becomes a specific political speculation itself: namely, Mamata Banerjee's own attempt to forge a privileged relationship with leading capitalist actors, bypassing the BJP central government, and to make West Bengal a prime destination for the global tech industry. In Cape Town, the smart city and the Silicon Cape projects emerge as terrains in which post-apartheid state actors negotiate their loyalty to a mission of social justice and inclusion with a neoliberal, pro-growth, and entrepreneurial mandate. Urban smartness is the discursive horizon in which contradictory initiatives are inscribed: the extensive rolling out of broadband infrastructures 'for digital inclusion' serves tech districts in the central city but leaves the townships underserviced; and digital training to township youth is only provided selectively, based on the entrepreneurial potential of the candidates.

More broadly, however, speculative urbanism is also a constellation of storylines, projects, and practices, through which a broad range of urban actors operationalise visions of future urban smartness in shaping the present. This includes, of course, real estate operations leveraging smart city projects, such as the new wave of developments around the Bengal Silicon Valley, or the market boom of Woodstock alongside the Silicon Cape clustering of startups. But there is more to it than financial speculations. There are, for example, the ways in which the middle-class residents of New Town identify and construct themselves as smart citizens, producing normative narratives of the urban space that stigmatise informal vendors and certain modes of being in public space. And, in parallel, municipal bylaws echo and build upon such discourses, banning hawkers from the parts of the city that must be branded as smart. Similarly, in Cape Town the smart city coincides with securitised, sanitised, and often racialised spaces, where the urban (visibly) poor are not welcome. As smart city narratives easily conflate with white middle-class anxieties of security, hygiene, and decency, the making of the smart city aligns with practices of social marginalisation and exclusion. The anticipation of certain urban futures—preparing for becoming hi-tech, innovative, efficient, global, and wealthy—translates into legitimising and cultivating only certain modes of being in the city, at the expense of others. In proposing this expanded and polysemic notion of speculative urbanism, my intention is not to dismiss the role of finance. On the contrary, I acknowledge that financial movements are critical to smart city projects, running from real estate, to the flows of capital across the tech industry. In the forms of urbanism discussed so far, however, speculation is more than merely economic because urban futures are envisioned, anticipated, mobilised, and performed at multiple levels and in multiple forms, from political discourses to lifestyles, from bylaws to educational initiatives. And such urban futures concern more than profits and investment returns, becoming part of urban and regional development strategies, government and policies, social aspirations, and modes of being in the city.

REFERENCES

Boiles-Leonard, V. (2023). *Substantive belonging in a post-apartheid city: Examining the intersection of race, class, space, and colonial legacies in Cape Town.* Doctoral dissertation, Carleton University.

Cameron, A. (2017, August 13). #Datamustfall: Poor locked out of the digital economy. *News24.* https://www.news24.com/fin24/datamustfall-poor-locked-out-of-the-digital-economy-20170811

Cape Town CBD gets smart with web technology. (2018, January 26). *Timeslive.* https://www.timeslive.co.za/news/sci-tech/2018-01-26-cape-town-cbd-gets-smart-with-web-technology/

Chatterjee, P. (2006). *The politics of the governed. Reflections on popular politics in most of the world.* Columbia University Press.

Chakraborti, S. (2022a, May 11). More land for Bengal Silicon Valley. *The Times of India.* https://timesofindia.indiatimes.com/city/kolkata/more-land-for-bengal-silicon-valley/articleshow/91478697.cms

Chakraborti, S. (2022b, June 6). New Town Kolkata development authority to make Silicon Valley hawker-free zone. *The Times of India.* https://timesofin dia.indiatimes.com/city/kolkata/new-town-kolkata-development-authority-to-make-silicon-valley-hawker-free-zone/articleshow/92030420.cms

Cirolia, L. R., & Harber, J. (2022). Urban statecraft: The governance of transport infrastructures in African cities. *Urban Studies, 59*(12), 2431–2450. https://doi.org/10.1177/00420980211055692

Datta, A. (2015). New urban utopias of postcolonial India: 'Entrepreneurial urbanization' in Dholera smart city, Gujarat. *Dialogues in Human Geography, 5*(1), 3–22. https://doi.org/10.1177/2043820614565748

Dey, I., Samaddar, R., & Sen, S. K. (2013). *Beyond Kolkata: Rajarhat and the dystopia of urban imagination.* Routledge India.

Didier, S., Peyroux, E., & Morange, M. (2012). The spreading of the city improvement district model in Johannesburg and Cape Town: Urban regeneration and the neoliberal agenda in South Africa. *International Journal of Urban and Regional Research, 36*(5), 915–935. https://doi.org/10.1111/j.1468-2427.2012.01136.x

Ferguson, J. (2010). The uses of neoliberalism. *Antipode, 41,* 166–184.

Ferguson, J. (2015). *Give a Man a Fish. Reflections on the New Politics of Distribution.* Duke University Press.

Fields, D. (2023). Speculative urbanism. *Environment and Planning a: Economy and Space, 55*(2), 511–516. https://doi.org/10.1177/0308518X2 21125473

Goldman, M. (2011). Speculative urbanism and the making of the next world city. *International Journal of Urban and Regional Research, 35*(3), 555–581. https://doi.org/10.1111/j.1468-2427.2010.01001.x

Ghosh, A., & Arora, B. (2021). Smart cities in India: Urban laboratory, paradigmatic city, or speculative urbanism? *Transactions of the Institute of British Geographers, 46*(3), 598–613. https://doi.org/10.1111/tran.12434

Interview 1. (May 2015). JS, NKT City manager, New Town [in person].

Interview 2. (December 2017). JS, NKT City manager [online].

Interview 3. (November 2017). MB, former intern at smart city consultancy firm in New Town [online].

Interview 4. (September 2016). PK. Female software engineer and leader of smart citizens group in New Town [online].

Interview 5. (November 2015). ZS, tech journalist and consultant, Cape Town [in person].

Interview 6. (November 2016). PDW, former city manager, Cape Town [in person].

Interview 7. (October 2018). MN, real estate analyst in Kolkata [online].
Interview 8. (November 2016). PV, former IT & development consultant, Cape Town. [in person].
Interview 9 (November 2016). KM, real estate operator, Cape Town [in person].
Interview 10. (November 2016). AG freelance tech journalist, Cape Town [in person].
Jasanoff, S. (2015). *The ethics of invention: Technology and the human future*. W.W. Norton & Company.
Kalia, R. (1990). *Bhubaneshwar: From a temple town to a capital city*. Southern Illinois University Press.
Kalia, R. (1997). *Chandigarh: The making of an Indian city*. Oxford University Press.
Kalia, R. (2004). *Gandhinagar: Building national identity in postcolonial India*. University of South Carolina Press.
Karvonen, A. (2020). Urban techno-politics: Knowing, governing, and imagining the city. *Science as Culture, 29*(3), 365–387. https://doi.org/10.1080/095 05431.2020.1766011
Leitner, H., & Sheppard, E. (2023). Unleashing speculative urbanism: Speculation and urban transformations. *Environment and Planning a: Economy and Space, 55*(2), 359–366. https://doi.org/10.1177/0308518X231151945
Mahadevan, S., & Naqvi, I. (2017). Contesting urban citizenship: The urban poor's strategies of state engagement in Chennai, India. *International Development Planning Review, 39*(1), 77–95.
Miller, T. R. (2020). Imaginaries of sustainability: The techno-politics of smart cities. *Science as Culture, 29*(3), 365–387. https://doi.org/10.1080/095 05431.2020.1766011
New Town Forum & News. (n.d.). *Facebook group*. Facebook. Retrieved [Date you accessed the page], from https://www.facebook.com/groups/206218 8457182060/
Parnell, S., & Robinson, J. (2012). (Re)theorizing cities from the Global South: Looking beyond neoliberalism. *Urban Geography, 33*(4), 593–617. https:// doi.org/10.2747/0272-3638.33.4.593
Personal Conversation 1. (November 2018). AC, member of New Town Facebook Group [online].
Personal Conversation 2. (November 2018). AG, member of New Town Facebook Group [online].
Personal Conversation 3. (November 2018). RS, member of New Town Facebook Group [online].
Pollio, A. (2019). Incubators at the frontiers of capital: An ethnographic encounter with startup weekend in Khayelitsha, Cape Town. *Annals of the American Association of Geographers, 110*(4), 1244–1259.

Pollio, A. (2020). Making the silicon cape of Africa: Tales, theories and the narration of startup urbanism. *Urban Studies, 57*(13), 2715–2732. https://doi.org/10.1177/0042098019884275

Pollio, A., & Cirolia, L. R. (2022). Fintech urbanism in the startup capital of Africa. *Journal of Cultural Economy, 15*(4), 508–523. https://doi.org/10.1080/17530350.2022.2058058

Property in New Town Kolkata. (n.d.). propotiger.com. https://www.proptiger.com/kolkata-real-estate/new-town-overview-51323

PWC, Wesgro & City of Cape Town. (2013). *Digital gateway to Africa. Cape Town's creative software design and development sector.* Sanec. http://www.sanec.org/themes/sanec/uploads/files/cape-town-digital-gateway-to-africa.pdf

Rao, U. (2013). Tolerated encroachment: Resettlement policies and the negotiation of the licit/Illicit divide in an Indian metropolis. *Cultural Anthropology, 28,* 760–779.

Ray Chaudhury, P. (2022). The political asceticism of Mamata Banerjee: Female populist leadership in contemporary India. *Politics & Gender, 18*(4), 942–977. https://doi.org/10.1017/S1743923X21000209

Rossi, U., & Di Bella, A. (2017). Startup urbanism: New York, Rio de Janeiro and the global urbanization of technology-based economies. *Environment and Planning a: Economy and Space, 49*(5), 999–1018. https://doi.org/10.1177/0308518X17690153

Rossiter, N. (2016). *Software, infrastructure, labor: A media theory of logistical nightmares.* Routledge.

Roy, A. (2009). Why India cannot plan its cities: Informality, insurgence and the idiom of urbanization. *Planning Theory, 8*(1), 76–87. https://doi.org/10.1177/1473095208099299

Roy, A., & Ong, A. (Eds.). (2011). *Worlding cities: Asian experiments and the art of being global.* Wiley-Blackwell.

Sadowski, J., & Bendor, R. (2019). Selling smartness: Corporate narratives and the smart city as a sociotechnical imaginary. *Science, Technology, & Human Values, 44*(3), 540–563. https://doi.org/10.1177/0162243918806061

Sepehr, P., & Felt, U. (2023). Urban imaginaries as tacit governing devices: The case of smart city Vienna. *Science, Technology, & Human Values.* https://doi.org/10.1177/01622439231178597

SAVCA (South Africa Venture Capital and Private Equity Association). (2017). *Private equity industry survey.* https://savca.co.za/wp-content/uploads/2017/06/SAVCA-2017-Private-Equity-Industry-Survey-electronic.pdf

Smart City Proposal. (2015). Retrieved from https://www.nkdamar.org/File/SCP%20New%20Town%20Kolkata_04042016_Draft%20Final.pdf

Startup Genome. (2021). *The Global Startup Ecosystem Report GSER 2021.* https://startupgenome.com/report/gser2021

2 SPECULATIVE URBANISM: TRANSFORMING THE PRESENT ...   57

State of Cape Town Report (2022). https://resource.capetown.gov.za/docume ntcentre/Documents/City%20research%20reports%20and%20review/SOCT_ Report_Summary_2022.pdf#page=3.00

von Schnitzler, A. (2016). *Democracy's infrastructure: Techno-politics and protest after apartheid.* Princeton University Press.

Tnn. (2018, November 3). IT biggies apply for 75 acres at New Town Silicon Valley. *The Times of India.* https://timesofindia.indiatimes.com/city/kol kata/it-biggies-apply-for-75-acres-at-new-town-silicon-valley/articleshow/ 66484192.cms

West Bengal with Rohit (2023a, December 17). *Bengal Silicon Valley Hub Rising, Latest Construction Updates—Kolkata's Tech Transformation Ep 314* [Video]. Youtube. https://www.youtube.com/watch?v=o6M8QzV_a8A

West Bengal with Rohit (2023b, April 30). *Walk to the Bengal Silicon Valley Hub, Kolkata with IAS Officer Mr Debashis Sen Ep 250.* [Video]. Youtube. https:// www.youtube.com/watch?v=s75T-d4IEoA

CHAPTER 3

Testbed Cities: Experiments, Prototypes, Trials

'Well, looking back now, I can say it was sort of a leap of faith... We knew it could be done, somehow, and we did it! We did great, I think. But definitely, it was a big experiment and a risk for everyone: for us, for SAP, and for the city' (Interview 11, 2016).

This is how MK, an IT consultant, begins the account of his experience with the implementation of the custom SAP[1] Enterprise Resource Planning (ERP) software for the City of Cape Town. Before launching his own firm, MK worked for several years with the City of Cape Town, implementing and managing specific modules of the software for municipal departments. Our conversation takes place in a cafeteria inside the busy Cape Town's international convention centre, where MK, now an established and well-known name in his field, is shortly going to give a talk at a corporate forum. But he was only a recent graduate when, in 2003, he was hired by an IT service provider to support the city in developing Project Ukuntinga, a holistic SAP software infrastructure integrating all the city's business processes into a single automated system. The stakes were very high, and pressure was intense, MK recalls. As part of its smart city strategy, the city had made the controversial decision to commit substantial resources (R300 million) on purchasing software

---

[1] SAP is a German multinational software company and the world's largest vendor of enterprise resource planning software.

© The Author(s), under exclusive license to Springer Nature Switzerland AG 2025
I. Antenucci, *Future-proofed*,
https://doi.org/10.1007/978-3-031-86429-2_3

59

and digitalising business processes while a large part of the population lacked essential services (Case Study: How SAP Runs Cape Town, 2013). As a result, MK and his colleagues were tasked with more than a merely technical job. At stake was proving that the political decision was right, 'that the experiment was going to be successful', turning the city bureaucracy into an efficient and cost-effective machine. They were aware to be sailing uncharted waters, managing the largest implementation of SAP for local government ever undertaken. The first step was integrating key functions from the Finance, Human Resources (HR), Billing, and Plant Maintenance departments, building sound foundations onto which other applications and operational layers could be added. Importantly, this initial stage passed the financial test: digitalisation quickly provided improved revenues for the city, with savings in the range of R100 million per year in the fields of IT maintenance, procurement, and HR management (Wright et al., 2023). Several more modules were then developed over time, such as land and property management in 2012, and transport in 2013. Eventually, SAP took over the entire back office of the city, integrating over 420 business processes across several departments, including healthcare, electricity, water sanitisation and transportation, housing, refuse collection, libraries, and more. Such results are very much the outcome of piecemeal, contingent experiments, as software applications designed for corporate operations had to be repurposed for delivering services to a city of 3.7 millions. Each new SAP module had to be customised, MK recalls, as both the software and the city's business processes needed to be translated, to some extent, to work together. City staff, from junior hires to senior management, had to be trained not only to use SAP functions, but also to understand the very premises of the process, i.e. what kind of data were going to be available to them through the software, and how data could be accessed and interpreted. As MK puts it, 'For a long time, every day was a new test, checking what was working and what was not. Every step, every new application, we had to tweak and fix something (*of the SAP original product, a/n*) to make it work, try and tweak and fix until it finally worked'. And even when everything finally came together, when the ERP system encapsulated all operations, the experiment was not over. 'This is the thing when you really want to leverage technologies: There's always something new, something better, something to upgrade. I think the City has done a great job so far (*with digitalisation, a/n*) but it's not over, technology moves on, there is so much more that can be done, that needs to be done. Just because the system works today, it doesn't mean it's good enough for tomorrow. You have to keep experimenting, or eventually you'll fall behind. It's never over' (Interview 11, 2016).

A few months before meeting MK in Cape Town, on a torrid afternoon, I was sitting in the lobby of the five-star Novotel in New Town Kolkata with DB, a senior city official who had served in major administrative bodies. He enthusiastically described the projects that were being drafted as first steps of the 'smart' city to come. My interlocutor was closely involved in the planning of smart New Town (at the time formally still in the application process) and agreed to give me an 'unofficial' interview after long email negotiations. That turned out to be the first of many conversations spanning over a few years, which provided me with valuable insights into the unfolding of smart city projects in New Town. The Novotel, an upmarket venue that DB suggested for our meeting, was not far from the offices of the New Town Kolkata Development Authority in New Town. The tall, glass-panelled building looked out to an unfinished rail flyover, a few more hotels, and several towers that were still under construction. Beyond the hotel's fences, vacant plots of land were filled with garbage and construction debris. Biswa Bangla Sarani, New Town's largest road, ran noisy and dusty, a few steps away from the hotel entrance. From the quiet of the hotel lobby I could spot, on the opposite side of the road, tea stalls packed with customers seeking shelter from the scorching sun. DB showed me pictures of the future city, in which the surroundings looked dramatically different from the present. Manicured parks instead of dumping grounds, brand new buildings, cycling paths, and, of course, sensors and computers everywhere, from bus stands to garbage bins. Proud and enthusiast, my interlocutor went on to illustrate the technologies that were supposed to transform the face of New Town. Information on routes and timetables of GPS-tracked public transport, including electric buses, *autos,* and *totos,* would be available on a mobile app. In smart parking areas, sensors would collect data from cars, allowing users to book and pay in advance for their parking with their phones. Sensors on drainage covers would record the quantity of rainfall and activate pumps automatically to avoid water logging. Waste-collection vehicles would also be tracked via GPS, while sensor-equipped public bins will send real-time alerts when full. All conventional meters for water and electricity would be replaced with smart meters allowing remote reading, monitoring of load profiles, and detection of potential tampering. Real-time data on power consumption would be shared with the police 'to keep special attention on vacant houses' and prevent illegal occupations (Smart City Proposal, 2015, p. 88). Light poles would be equipped with sensors that monitor air pollution, CCTV cameras performing 24/7 surveillance, and panic buttons connected to emergency response. The video content would then be analysed in real-time with image detection and facial recognition techniques. 'We will not spy on people, but we will know everything about the city', DB said fervently to conclude his review of smart city projects. 'We will have the real data. We will know if buses run late, if garbage bins are full, if someone feels sick on the street, everything' (Interview 12, 2015). By 'we', my interlocutor meant a somewhat unclear entity, loosely assembling local authorities, technical and administrative staff in charge of urban infrastructures, and the software itself.

Almost ten years later, the city described by DB, which accurately reflects the projects presented in the Smart City Proposal of 2015, does not exist yet. At the time of our conversation, almost all the planned infrastructures were still only on paper. As I am writing, in April 2023, some of them, such as sensing street lighting, CCTVs with real-time analytics, smart parking systems, smart bus shelters, and a few more, have been built, at least as trials. In contrast with the holistic urban system described by DB, and shown in the application pictures, the present of 'smart' New Town is made of piecemeal pilot projects, largely disconnected from one another. In a later conversation (Interview 13, 2018), DB emphasised the importance of testing as a key method for translating 'smart' city visions and plans into reality. The Area Based Development in New Town was specifically designed as a testbed for the broader 'smart' city plan: a portion of the city, named Action Area 1, in which new solutions could be trialled and evaluated, to create models that could then be replicated at the city scale (Smart City Proposal 2015, p. 24). Thus, several small pilot projects, not necessarily integrated with one another, have been carried out in the Area Based Development testbed, with the purpose to assess their viability, effects, and replicability. As DB noted, 'The project is there and it is an excellent one. But a project is a project. At the end of the day, we do not know what will work and what will not in reality. So we have to try things, and learn, and fix, and adjust. Sometimes the project will need to be amended if something doesn't work in real life. You know, Rome wasn't built in a day. You have to start somewhere' (Interview 13, 2018). These remarks suggest that these trials and pilots of technologies are far from formal, scientific tests, based on protocols and specific rules. Rather, they are inductively assessed to determine 'what works and what doesn't', to adapt the masterplan to the context and its contingencies, and to better calibrate the next steps.

These two ethnographic sketches frame the experimental nature of smart city initiatives, where normative visions of urban futures take shape (or don't) through testing and trialling, tweaking and fixing. New Town and Cape Town are testbeds for projects and infrastructures that are never completed, but incessantly amended and updated. The previous chapter of this book has explored forms of speculative urbanism in which narratives of urban futures are mobilised to shape and govern the present. In documenting smart experiments in New Town and Cape Town, this chapter delves into another nuance of urban speculations—the work of materialising the future, while postponing it constantly at the same time, through tests and trials. Far from hollow, the testbed condition is dense with socio-political effects, transforming the parameters and setting new rules for the urban milieu. Following Harriet Bulkeley and Vanesa Castán Broto (2013), I do not refer to experiments 'in the formal scientific sense of the term but rather to signify purposive interventions in which there is a more or less explicit attempt to innovate, learn or gain experience' (p. 363). Variously assembled under different contingencies, experiments, tests, and trials are nevertheless producing new spatial and socio-technical configurations in the urban space and introducing new political rationalities. This chapter opens by engaging with recent literature on testing as a socio-political practice, drawing out useful concepts and methods to make sense of smart urbanism in New Town and Cape Town. Two case studies follow: an experiment with drones for urban surveillance in New Town, and the implementation of the ERP system for the City of Cape Town, with a focus on its mobilisation in the water crisis of 2016/2018.

TESTBEDS AND TESTS

In recent years, testing and experimenting have been identified as modes of (urban) governance in different threads of scholarship. In their research on the greenfield smart city project of Songdo, in South Korea, Orit Halpern, Jess LeCavalier, Nerea Calvillo, and Wolfgang Pietsch (2013) speak of 'testbed urbanism' as a way of producing and governing urban territories. The smart city, they claim, is an engine for continuous growth, fuelled by tests and trials of new computing technologies and management strategies. Similarly to urban utopias of the past, such as Francis Bacon's New Atlantis, Halpern and colleagues note that this new vision of the city is also driven by an experimental logic, striving to achieve new forms of life and urban government. Yet, the smart city's epistemology substantially differs from that of the Enlightenment age, in that it seeks not to *represent* reality as accurately as possible, and according to specific rules, but rather to *produce* and *transform* 'territory, population, truth, and risk, with implications for representative government, subjectivity, and urban form'. The testbed is 'both literally and conceptually incomplete' (2013, p. 275), as the smart city is not conceived to ever reach completion, or settle into a final form. Instead, the smart infrastructures need to be continuously updated through more data and new computing techniques. For Halpern and colleagues, such continuous testing is precisely the point of smart city projects, insofar as it produces new protocols that can be sold and replicated. For this reason, the experiment is never meant to end. Albeit forged through the case study of Songdo, the concept of testbed urbanism speaks of global configurations of infrastructures and governance that are increasingly visible in urban projects and beyond. If not greenfield developments, New Town Kolkata and Cape Town are still testbeds, in which smart city projects are engrafting on complex urban histories, and technologies are seen as solutions to old and new urban problems. As smart experiments hit the ground, they produce not only a new urban territory, but new forms of urban subjectivities as well. And as the final form of the smart city remains nebulous and ever postponed, a patchwork of tests and trials becomes the terrain in which novel forms of governmentality take shape.

For Harriet Bulkeley and colleagues (2019), who studied living laboratories for sustainability transitions in European cities, it is the dynamics between control and contingency that defines urban experiments as a specific form of governance. Drawing on 40 case studies across Europe, Bulkeley, and colleagues sort the dispositions of laboratories into trials, enclaves, demonstrations, and platforms, based on the balance between control—predominant in trials—and contingency—which prevails in platforms. Such classification is perhaps too rigid for both New Town and Cape Town, where smart experiments combine traits of all the categories above, but do not fall neatly into any of those. Equally important, an analytical framework forged through European case studies solely cannot be straightforwardly applied to different geopolitical contexts. Yet Bulkeley and colleagues invitation to think through control and contingency proves useful in grasping the power dynamics at work through smart city experiments in New Town and Cape Town, and the ways in which the testing of technologies activates new forms of urban governmentality. In their recent work on testing, Noortje Marres and David Stark (2020) propose that continuous innovations in computing technologies have changed both the logic and the rules of testing as a practice, along with their societal implications. Tests have moved to the very core of social life. It is not so much that scientific tests have expanded beyond the boundaries of laboratories and into social environments. Rather, for Marres and Stark social environments have become the very object of testing, and testing has turned into a form of social engineering. The purpose of testing has indeed shifted from observing a certain process within given, controlled settings, to observing to what extent and how a certain process can transform the settings themselves. For example, big platforms such as Google, Facebook, Twitter, Uber, and the like, consistently run tests about social relations, communications, and emotions, across their far-reaching computing infrastructures (Marres & Stark, 2020). They do so because learning how to manage and possibly manipulate relations and emotions through algorithms is vital to platform capitalism. Tinkering with the settings of the social environment with the purpose of modifying human and non-human behaviours is exactly what platforms do. But this angle is strongly relevant also to the ways in which tests of smart technologies are reconfiguring urban environments. If big platforms offer striking examples of social engineering, the making of smart cities, as environments running on data capture, analysis, and feedback, is another terrain where testing becomes ubiquitous and incessant, and where it generates appreciable societal effects. As the remainder of this chapter illustrates, the testing of smart technologies in New Town and Cape Town unfolds, at the same time, as a process of urban (re)development. Tests generate new infrastructural forms, both material and immaterial, which reconfigure the ways in which the urban environment can be experienced. In so doing, tests change the rules of urban living, dictating new patterns of attention and control, including of the self.

Researching tests and testbeds empirically presents limits that must be reckoned with. Tests as research 'objects' can be elusive, shifting, and hardly accessible. This is particularly the case when, as in New Town and Cape Town, tests are conducted not as formal scientific undertakings, but informally, as practices aimed at making something work. Drawing the spatial and temporal boundaries of such tests is challenging, if not impossible. In my case studies, accurate information about where and when a specific test started or ended, how many participants were involved, which methods were used, and what the results are, were generally not available. This is in part because the tests I researched were open-ended, mutable by design, and meant to be amended and updated in progress. In both New Town and Cape Town, the tests are run by local institutional actors, like the New Town Kolkata Development Authority and the City of Cape Town, in partnership with private consultants and service providers. The details of such partnerships often remain, at least to some extent, undisclosed. A spectrum of elements, ranging from non-disclosure agreements to the political sensitivity of some information, to the restraint and wariness of the people involved, contribute to making the agreements and procedures of the tests quite opaque. Conscious of these limitations, in this chapter I seek to chart the tangible effects of testing *in* and *on* urban environments while registering their inherent instability and contingent nature. To do this, the next two sections review two experiments with 'smart' infrastructures that are taking place in New Town and Cape Town, the socio-economic contingencies in which they unfold, the technological properties that they carry, and some of their graspable effects on the urban environment.

DRONES

During the Covid-19 pandemic, drones were introduced in New Town to monitor the urban territory and to enforce lockdown restrictions (New Town Green City, 2022). The drones, provided by local tech company Kesowa of Federal Synergies India were used to survey 14 markets (10 community markets and 4 informal markets), 48 green verges, and other areas like shopping malls or campuses, to prevent people from gathering. Besides, drones were sent to verify alerts of overcrowding raised by the citizens through New Town's 24 × 7 help line or through the Neighbourhood Volunteering Groups constituted during the pandemic. Operating for 5 hours a day in two shifts—from 6.30 to 9.30 am and from 5.00 to 7.00 pm—drones would send real-time alerts of overcrowding to the New Town Kolkata Development Authority and to the police. According to the New Town Kolkata Development Authority, the experiment was very successful in achieving what ordinary patrolling was not able to achieve at the time: making people abide by social distancing measures. Apparently, New Town residents would not follow the recommendations of municipal and police officers, but this new layer of surveillance from above made it easier for law enforcement to detect and disperse crowds.

Having found the technology successful, the partnership between New Town Kolkata Development Authority and Kesowa gave life to another test. After the emergency phase of Covid-19 was over, in April 2021 a Drone & Drone Data Call Centre was set up in New Town, 'to help improve governance with actionable insights' (Interview 14, 2021). For my interlocutor DB, senior urban management in New Town was overall positively impressed by the results of the drone experiment during the lockdown, and interested in exploring more opportunities for using drones. At the same time, Kesowa was looking for institutional connections and visibility: New Town was a good arena to 'bring its technologies into the spotlight', as DB puts it. The company markets indeed a wide range of drone solutions, from the collection and processing of geospatial information to material tasks such as spraying fertilisers or repellents, or delivering items. Alongside enthusiasm, however, New Town governance also expressed some caution around relying on drones: the New Town Kolkata Development Authority chairman made it clear that drone providers had to prove the financial benefits of the solution, or 'it makes no sense to use a drone to do something a car can'. In other words, the drone test was shaped by two concurrent logics. On the one hand, the New Town Kolkata Development Authority had an interest in testing 'innovative technologies that would really make urban governance smarter' and put New Town 'ahead in the game' of smart cities (Interview 14, 2021). On the other hand, Kesowa, as a commercial provider, was trying to showcase their products and prove their worth to potential buyers. The Drone & Drone Data Call centre project consisted in establishing a local drone port which would provide on-demand services to both institutional clients and ordinary citizens; theoretically, anyone could call and request a drone mission to gather aerial data or deliver something critical. The New Town project report was titled, significantly, 'Re-active to Pro-Active governance', and solemnly announced how data sourced via Aerial Reconnaissance Units (ARU) could usher a new era of effective and transparent decision-making based on, verbatim, '"the Truth" for what it is' (Kesowa, 2021).

The urban data collected by drones—aerial pictures, maps, 3Ds—were stored and processed in a proprietary cloud, described as a 'dedicated single repository of information which can become a factual single source of truth' (Kesowa, 2021). In fact, drones are deployed mostly on missions of urban surveillance, monitoring roads and water bodies. Their task is to detect potential safety issues, such as holes in the roads, obstructions in water bodies, illegal waste dumping, stubble burning, or water stagnation, and send alerts to the New Town Kolkata Development Authority. In so doing, drones enable a chain of proactive and preemptive measures, which aim at intervening before the issue escalates into an emergency. For example, the health department is informed of polluted water bodies or garbage spots and may take action before a disease breaks out. The influx of real-time data and alerts changed the pace of urban governance: 'rather than spending a lot of time looking for potential problems, thus wasting valuable time for fixing them before it's too late, now we are informed of problems immediately, so we can devote all the time and resources to fixing them. Rather than responding to emergencies, we can anticipate them. This is the real added value. Of course, drones are not cheap, but how much money are they saving us?'. The added value is not merely financial, for DB, but even more appreciable in terms of image and public opinion. The administration can act more efficiently, and people perceive that: 'They see that we are on top of things, no more chasing problems, that we are in control, that we take action on issues when they are still minor and we do not let them escalate into a crisis' (Interview 14, 2021).

Significantly, drones are also used for stopping 'encroachments', a denigratory term describing informal dwellings and hawkers shops, which fit uneasily in the spaces of the 'smart' city. In the previous chapter, we have seen already how the presence of hawkers in public spaces is a point of friction between different classes and urban aspirations. In particular, urban planners and middle-class residents who have embraced smart city futures as corporate-oriented, upscale, and sanitised, advocate for the 'cleaning up' of informal vendors and dwellers. By collecting aerial geospatial data, drones make it possible to measure and quantify the presence of hawkers to a level of detail that was not achievable by older forms of patrolling. As DB explains, the police or the New Town Kolkata Development Authority units that used to be deployed to monitor hawkers were never able to cover the whole area at once, and to have 'the full picture, the whole map' of encroachments in New Town (Interview 14, 2021). So even if sanctions and evictions were enforced, the lack of spatial data and control would create a buffer that would allow hawkers to simply relocate elsewhere, until the next clearance. That might change thanks to the drones, DB argues, as the bird-eye view and the real-time data potentially make sure 'there is no more shelter, nowhere to hide for the encroachers'. For the New Town Kolkata Development Authority, encroachments are not only a problem in terms of aesthetics and image of the city, but a matter of security in the first place. DB spells out several of the risk factors attached to the presence of hawkers: their stalls obstruct pavements, making it unsafe for pedestrians to walk around; they attract roadside crowds, which are a cause of car accidents; they unduly dump garbage around, which poses a threat to public health; and they are sometimes linked to local syndicates or gangs, which engage in illegal activities. Interestingly, DB also notes that, by occupying public space that is formally designed for other purposes, or merely to remain empty, encroachments make it harder to survey and control the urban space. By filling spaces on roads, pavements, or green spots with makeshift facilities, goods, humans, animals, and waste, hawkers make it harder for urban authorities to get accurate data about those portions of the city. 'We have protocols in place for monitoring the conditions of roads and pavements, for the safety of everyone, but how can we do that if they block the roads? We want to monitor water bodies and green spots of the city for pollution and pest control, but we can't do that if they encroach'. Sometimes, if those areas have been equipped with sensors or other smart devices, the presence of hawkers—inadvertently or not—disrupts their functioning. As DB comments with indignation, 'We are striving to build a city with state-of-the-art technology, a city that is innovative, but they don't understand the technology, they tamper with it, they boycott'. In other words, 'encroachments' make the urban space less legible, especially in terms of data, and thus less computable. This is, for DB, a threat to the very future of the city. In the hopes of the city authority, it is also what drones are going to change, with their unescapable aerial gaze. Even more than enabling the evictions of hawkers, drones are entrusted with a preemptive effect, which would make evictions unnecessary. The regular presence of drones is expected to discourage people from setting up unauthorised dwellings and shops, 'like it happened during the pandemics', thus reducing the need for police intervention, 'avoiding confrontations', and saving time resources for local authorities (Interview 13, 2018). But as DB admits, even with the use of drones, the goal of making New Town an encroachment-free zone is still far away. Being only in the first stage of experimenting with the new technology, 'we can't expect immediate results. We will get there. We need more tests, and we need time for the city to adjust to these new methods' (Interview 14, 2021).

The testing of drones brings into view (literally) the contradictions at the heart of New Town's development: experiments with advanced computing technologies take place alongside the enduring, albeit undesired by many, presence of informal economies and urban poverty. Rather than acknowledging and addressing the socio-political causes of these phenomena, the smart city framework poses them as security concerns that need to be removed. And, with a distinct techno-solutionist approach, New Town government entrusts new automated infrastructures to finally accomplish what traditional methods and political negotiations could not thus far: making poverty disappear from the new smart city.

Automating the City

If the smart infrastructures of New Town Kolkata are largely still on paper or under construction, computing systems have been around in Cape Town for some time now. Cape Town has no smart city masterplan, like Pan City and the 'Area Based Development' of New Town, but a Smart City Strategy that more broadly encompasses urban digital development across the five pillars of leadership, policy, e-government, city/people development, and e-governance. In parallel, a dynamic digital industry has made a smart cluster of the city, filling it with new projects and products. Yet if Cape Town teems with smart devices and services of many sorts, the most consequential among digital infrastructures remains largely invisible to most. The city's ERP software, provided by SAP, currently handles almost the totality of business processes across several departments. Getting there, however, required multiple steps of testing and trialling for each building block or function. In absence of comprehensive examples of city-wide ERP programmes to draw upon, each added module had to be somehow crafted by customising applications used in corporate environments. MK recalls long meetings with city managers to learn the key elements of the procedures, and what was really needed in terms of software operations. He also observes how city managers were encouraged to rethink the business processes they were accustomed to, figuring out ways in which they could be improved and optimised through automation (Interview 11, 2016). For Wright et al. (2023), 'the focus of the project was on business process re-engineering'. In other words, city operatives were asked not to take technology for granted, as a ready-made solution, but rather to shift their mindset towards the technology, to try and think 'like the software'. Once the settings and parameters of business processes had been re-evaluated in the light of the opportunities provided by SAP modules—such as having access to real-time information across several departments—the revised processes were then encoded and automated into SAP software. The brainstorming phase was thus followed by a series of experiments, in which IT consultants like MK tried to translate content into code and software applications. The team would select 'existing applications that looked suitable', and tried to tweak here and there to meet the city's requirements for that particular task. The developers would then train city staff on the new software modules, and start a trial period to see what was working and what still needed improving. In the first phase of the project, the benchmark was primarily financial: the test needed to prove not only sustainable, but profitable for the city's budget. As André Steltzner, former Chief Information Officer of the City of Cape Town, makes clear, the first and foremost target of the ERP software was to 'drive value' in appreciable measure, to justify the expenditure incurred as well as claims for future investments in digitalisation (Howlett, 2013).

With the integration of more data and applications from different departments, the opportunity to create a single record of each citizen or household, as needed, came into view. For MK, 'that (to have a 360 view of each citizen and household, a/n) might have been the desire and hope of some City officials since the beginning', but it was never formalised as an official goal of the project, 'until one day we realised that we were there already, that we had gathered and integrated enough information' (Interview 11, 2016). The conversation then shifted from how to combine previously siloed datasets to how to make the most of the data available in real-time. Trial by trial, a system of analytics running across different datasets, such as employment history, income levels, water and electricity consumption, social payments received, and more, began to take shape. SAP algorithms track individual and household interactions with the city, sorting them into different classes of 'risk'—whereby risk can be defined by unpaid bills, chronic unemployment, and other indicators of vulnerability, which might place a financial burden on the city budget. This automated profiling quickly resulted in a novel mode of proactive and preemptive urban governance. City managers claim to be able to identify needs and vulnerabilities more accurately, and to detect potential frauds, thus saving time and money for the municipality. For example, households that are profiled as low-income and potentially unable to pay for services, are offered discounted rates. This, Steltzner notes, is less expensive for the city than enforcing debt collection. As Steltzner makes clear, however, making people feel that the city has an accurate, comprehensive view of them is also an effective preemptive strategy, in that it discourages unruly behaviours (Howlett, 2013).

The novel data-driven approach was leveraged by the city in the 2016–2018 water crisis. Since 2015, Cape Town has faced long droughts and the worst water crisis in its history. As the levels of dams and reservoirs continued to go down, severe restrictions were enforced on water consumption. The city strategy to avoid Day Zero—the day in which the city dam would fall below 13.5%, leading to radical water rationing—was shaped, as Millington and Scheba (2021) argue, by the concurrent imperatives to avert a social disaster while remaining financially solvent. In the absence of an off-the-shelf disaster plan, the city had to experiment new solutions step by step. The capability to process and share real-time data across different departments turned out to be critical to the city's response. This was a test in the test—that is, putting technologies that were still being trialled at work in managing an unprecedented urban crisis. Approximately 220.000 smart water meters, officially known as Water Management Devices (WMDs), were installed, especially in indigent households. Those are the digital evolution of the controversial prepaid meters (von Schnitzler, 2008), already in use since the early 2000s to watch and discipline water consumption among the urban poor—typically low-income black families that consumed more water than they could pay for. But unlike their predecessors, smart meters send real-time data on water usage in each household, and automatically switch off when the daily limit has been reached. As the water crisis escalated, smart meters were also made available to assist non-indigent households in saving water. The city combined real-time data on domestic usage sent by smart meters with data on dam storage and pipe condition to produce risk models of water levels and daily consumption. Such models would drive decisions around further water restrictions to be enforced to prevent Day Zero, as well as disaster planning, such as measures to ensure essential water provision to the population in case of critical shortage. Day Zero—the day when taps would shut down—was in fact a risk model itself, a date calculated on the ratio between average daily water consumption and the number of users, which was postponed several times and eventually cancelled in March 2018. At the same time, real-time data were used to set up a public Water Dashboard and a Water Usage Map, as part of the #DayZero campaign for citizen education and engagement. If the dashboard informed the public about dam storage, changes in water levels, and the amount of water production on a daily basis, the usage map, based on the city's billing data, displayed household and neighbourhood water usage. Virtuous households, whose consumption levels were exceptionally low, were awarded a green dot. Admittedly, the map was designed to enable 'peer-to-peer monitoring and competition' (Wright et al., 2023, p. 37). For some observers, the strategy was more effective in inducing behavioural changes and curbing water consumption than changes in tariffs (2023, p. 38).

As this brief review suggests, the progressive testing and introduction of the ERP platform in the City of Cape Town turned out to be about much more than merely streamlining data and procedures. The process of trying new digital solutions and automating services gradually changed the very rationale and settings of municipal governance towards 'thinking like the software'. If cost-effectiveness was the imperative leading software operations in the first phase, that quickly shifted towards placing data and data-driven decisions at the core of urban governance. As a result, the provision of municipal services has become subject to algorithmic scrutiny, scoring, and validation. This algorithmic apparatus is in fact dense with political implications, beginning with its supposed neutrality and objectivity. As former City CIO Andre Stelzner significantly declared in an interview: 'SAP's core value is that it provides a set of procedures that the council and its employees follow to run the city' so that 'from a political perspective, there is not much scope for radical change, since the way the city operates is encoded into the SAP system' (Case Study: How SAP Runs Cape Town, 2013). In other words, for Stelzner, managing a city by using procedures that are encoded in corporate software makes politics irrelevant. This suggests that critical decisions around socio-economic issues, such as the provision of basic utilities and measures for poverty relief, which the City is responsible for, are potentially removed from political negotiations and debates, and merely computed based on cost-effectiveness criteria.

Testing (as) Urban Governance

Urban experiments with smart technologies are fundamentally speculative socio-technical processes (Bulkeley & Castán Broto, 2013) which are tasked with projecting urban futures in the present. They are critical for crafting imaginaries of the city to come, for building networks of knowledge-power—such as the public-private partnerships between urban government and tech providers—and for sedimenting new practices and norms of urban living. Even if contained within certain boundaries of time and space—think of the drone trial, or of the Water Dashboard—experiments are not marginal in terms of the broader effects they produce. Rather, they bring into view, and into action, new forms of control and authority over urban space, be those drone surveillance or real-time data on water consumption. And far from operating as open-ended, learning processes, smart experiments appear to be bounded by specific interests and strategies, whether to curb encroachments, or to avert an environmental disaster. Assembling these elements, and following Marres and Stark (2020), I am interested in understanding how smart tests are *changing the settings* of urban environments, and thus of the ways in which cities are experienced, known, and governed. While a more complete spectrum of these modifications will only be appreciable over time, I argue that two key processes are already visible.

I. *Crafting Smart Citizens*

The first concerns the ways in which citizens perceive and conduct themselves. Tests activate novel understandings of the urban environment and of how to be in it. From conversations with two consultants who worked with the New Town Kolkata Development Authority on the development of smart projects I learned that, for them, one key aspect of testing infrastructures is about educating citizens about 'smartness' and generating new modes of being the city. As one consultant reported, 'Smart cities are made of smart people. You have to educate citizens to interact with such technologies (..) not just technically, but morally. They need to become familiar, to trust. Then you will get results' (Interview 15, 2015). By results, I understood from broader conversations, they meant citizens becoming willing and capable to share their data, to interact 'productively', rather than 'sceptically' or 'destructively'

(Interview 18, 2015) with the new technologies, to trust the new infrastructures as carriers of some form of superior knowledge and authority, and to act accordingly. Both consultants emphasised time and again how, in their experience, the close and continued interaction with smart technologies steadily transformed people's mindset and habits, steering them towards practices and principles of 'smart' citizenship' (Interview 16, 2018; Interview 19, 2023). Pedagogical effects stemmed from experiments with data-driven governance in Cape Town as well, and especially from the water crisis management. Here, the public use of data and algorithmic predictions was effective in transforming the behaviour of citizens and their relationship with water consumption in the face of the draught. FK, an IT and management analyst, who at the time of the interview had been consulting for the City of Cape Town over the previous decade, argues that 'the fact itself of possessing and displaying the data holds an educational power' and can affect people's approach and conduct (Interview 20, 2019). It is not so much a matter of predicting the future, but rather of showing that the city has the technological capability to know things better and faster than the average citizen. My interlocutor locates a key pedagogical element in this differential of power between urban authorities and dwellers. Regardless of the accuracy of the predictive models involved, the very act of displaying a holistic view of water availability, and of patterns of consumption by household, was already highly performative in shifting 'the collective perception and mindset' around the water crisis and perhaps, more broadly, around resources and environmental awareness in general. The educational implications of the testing of smart infrastructures resonates with Alberto Vanolo's idea of 'smartmentality' (2014), which describes how the smart city operates as a governmental strategy producing distinct forms of urban subjectivities. More than merely technologically literate, smart citizens are willing to comply with, and to co-produce, a specific agenda of urban remaking pivoted around neoliberal versions of environmentalism and care. Similarly, for the IT consultants who helped define New Town's smart city plans, smart citizenship means 'many things, not only (being) tech-savvy, but responsible and civic-minded' (Interview 15, 2015). And for the brains behind the digitalisation of Cape Town, 'a city is only as smart as its citizens, which means that technology will only be really effective when new principles and new values (*of citizenship*, a/n) have settled' (Interview 20, 2019). In other words, tests are seen as performative processes, which probe not only the technical operations of new infrastructures, but also the ways in which new codes of conduct and new modes of being in the city emerge. In the hopes of smart city planners, as new technologies are tested, citizens will recast themselves and their ordinary practices to interact with the new devices. As drones fly over New Town, they are performing not only tasks of surveillance and risk assessment, but also the visualisation of 'smart' security and urban government. And as dashboards of urban data in Cape Town display patterns of behaviours, they are also presenting a new moral regime of civic responsibility and (self) vigilance.

As part of their work with New Town Kolkata Development Authority, the consultants I interviewed regularly run meetings with New Town residents to investigate and assess how the city is responding to the introduction of smart technologies. They have found that the drones experiment has been so far a successful example of 'smart' urbanity. According to the consultants, people in New Town have come to trust the drones as security carriers, 'something that improves the safety of the city', by ensuring that potential issues will be detected and acted upon quickly (Interview 17, 2023; Interview 19, 2023). More importantly, drones seem to have induced a self-disciplining effect. As a result, the consultants report, people are more conscious about their own behaviours, as well as of the urban environment they live in. Not only do they restrain from doing something wrong, such as dumping waste or burning stubble, 'because they know they are being watched' (Interview 17, 2023), they also, and more significantly, perceive that they live in an urban environment that is safer, efficient, and trustworthy, and which therefore 'deserves' their commitment to be vigilant and compliant citizens. Yet so far drones seem to be less efficient in doing what they were originally deployed for, such as preventing 'encroachments'. Hawkers seem to react to aerial surveillance merely by moving their settlements to other areas of the city, until the next round of inspection spots them. There is no indication, so far, of informal dwellers having interiorised the new epistemologies and practices of citizenship brought on by smart technologies, which middle-class residents are eager to express. In other words, the processes of urban subjectivation activated by the testing of smart technologies seem to bear the same socio-spatial boundaries that pertain to the smart city initiative as a whole. Middle-class residents are deliberately involved by urban authorities in the introduction of smart technologies, at least to some extent, and appear largely responsive, often actively engaging with those. Meanwhile, not only are residents from the informal sector marginalised in planning processes, they are also positioned as passive recipients, or even, as in the drone experiment, explicitly as *targets* of smart technologies. In Cape Town, experiments with smart technologies as part of a broader campaign for managing the water crisis have also produced appreciable shifts in mindsets and practices of citizenship. For FK, who has closely observed and assessed the development of the water crisis, and of the measures undertaken to avert it, the public data-driven approach adopted by the city has been 'a game changer' (Interview 20, 2019). It is not only, and not so much, about inducing or coercing people to consume less water, such as by raising tariffs or enforcing restrictions, it is mostly about creating new knowledge, a new way of looking at resources, and 'a new sense of belonging to the city, of doing your bit'. If that could have been the case with any successful communication campaign, data and predictive models were critical, FK recounts, for offering an authoritative source of information, of truth. People might not trust politicians, who are known for being corrupted and for manipulating information for their own interests. But many felt that they could trust the data as 'objective and above all parties'. (Apparently, the fact that data could still be manipulated by politicians was not a matter of concern). For FK, the biggest success of the strategy, beyond avoiding an environmental disaster, was proposing a new, 'smart', way of seeing the city, its resources, and the role of citizens in it. 'It was not only about cancelling Day Zero, but even more about showing that with data and cutting-edge technologies we *can* have better governance. But we must be ready to play our part, to learn and change'. Yet here, similarly to New Town, this process of urban subjectivation seems to be filtered by socio-spatial factors. As FK admits, his enthusiastic account of new smart citizens was largely based on information from middle to high-income families, living either in the City Bowl or in residential suburbs. Township residents were, in FK's words, 'not so collaborative and forthcoming' in sharing their experience, and way more sceptical about the potential of new technologies (Interview 20, 2019). Although low-income households did comply to water restrictions as much as middle- and high-income ones (Matikinca et al., 2020), to most of them, the main effect of the Day Zero campaign was the fear of losing access to water. Many also complained about the loss of livelihoods, as in the case of households who could no longer grow vegetables to eat or sell.

In conclusion, the testing of smart technologies contributes to the production of new urban subjectivities. The introduction of real-time monitoring systems, such as water dashboards or surveillance drones, does more than optimising resource management or enhance security; it also instils a sense of continuous oversight among residents, as well as new hierarchies of worth and importance in the urban environment. The experiments reconfigure the ways in which urban residents perceive themselves and their roles within the city, but in ways that are unevenly informed by socio-spatial conditions. For middle-class residents, smart experiments are not merely about adapting to new tools but mostly about internalising a new rationality that emphasises trust in data-driven decisions, individual responsibility, and self-regulation. The knowledge that urban matters, as well as specific individual conducts, are being tracked and analysed by intelligent systems, engages citizens into self-disciplining practices and gives shape to novel forms of algorithmic authority. At the same time, low-income and marginalised residents perceive the new technologies more passively, sceptically, or negatively, as victims or targets.

II. *A New Distribution of the Sensible: Shifting Patterns of Attention and Normativity*

The second effect of smart testing consists in producing new configurations of infrastructures that condition the ways in which things are perceived and measured in urban environments. Experiments make certain behaviours, spaces, and populations hyper-surveyed under the gaze of smart technologies, while others remain unseen or marginalised: as a result, new urban regimes of visibility and invisibility take form. Drones, for instance, put the focus on informal encroachments as illegal practices; at the same time, the precarious living conditions of a large part of the population—the poor, the displaced, the migrants—are deliberately kept out of the picture. This selective visibility is, of course, far from neutral, and aligned with a smart city agenda in which the enforcement of order, control, and efficiency—or at least the semblance of it—are privileged over pursuing equity and social justice. In the water dashboard example, we see how data on water consumption are made hyper-visible, and publicly awarded or sanctioned, whereas the sharp socio-economic gaps between households—i.e. between those who can afford to dig boreholes in their own property, for example, and those who need to queue to fill their jugs at public fountains—remain hidden.

Borrowing from Jacques Rancière, I argue that tests of smart technologies produce 'a new distribution of the sensible' in urban environments. In his book, *The Politics of Aesthetics* (2004), Rancière argues that any social order is constructed through a specific distribution (or partition) of the sensible. This concept illustrates how distinct modes of perception set the boundaries between what can be seen or not seen, said or not said, heard or not heard, measured or not measured, and, ultimately, between what is licit or illicit. Rancière describes social roles and forms of participation that are defined through specific distributions of the sensible, which can at once include and exclude. Through a detailed examination of historical examples of the politics of the aesthetic, Rancière maintains that every social and political system is first of all an aesthetic regime—where the term 'aesthetic' refers to what is experienced through the senses—insofar as it is organised through distinct forms of perception and the sensorial relations between humans, objects, and nature. Here, I appropriate the notion of the distribution of the sensible and put it to work in a very different context, to read how tests of smart technologies are reconfiguring urban life. In so doing, I pair the concept with others that grasp the generative power of technologies as they unfold in context. One is Jennifer Gabrys' idea of digital ontogenesis, whereby sensors—and, I argue, other digital devices—do not merely connect, or mediate between, discrete entities, but produce 'medial relationships that are world-making and world-sustaining' (Gabrys, 2016, p. 263). Drawing on the work of Gilbert Simondon and Alfred North Whitehead, Gabrys sees sensing infrastructures as 'in-forming', that is, capable of giving form to and informing experiences. Expanding on this line of thinking, and especially on Simondon's account of technology as ontogenesis, Thomas Keating (2024) proposes the notion of techno-genesis to highlight the autonomous, creative, and determining power of technologies to unfold and generate new relational forms. Back to our case studies, I argue that smart experiments are techno-genetic, processes, in that they reconfigure sensorial experiences in ways that produce at once new urban spatialities (Leszczynski, 2015) and new modes of being in the city. A second concept that is critical to situate Rancière's distribution of the sensible in this analysis of urban testbeds is Keller Easterling's infrastructural power (2014). For Easterling, infrastructures—be they the planning standards of the corporate free zone or, closer to our topic, broadband networks and its corollaries—possess their own agency and dispositions, which shape and dictate the rules of space and life around them. Far from being a mere tool in the hands of humans, infrastructures are constantly doing something *in* and *to* the city—something that might be different from their declared purpose. If we use these lenses to read the tests discussed in this chapter, we can see how the introduction of smart technologies is not only shifting notions and practices of citizenship, but also enabling, constraining, or disabling, certain forms of perception and interaction, making certain things possible or impossible.

Devices like drones, water meters, or dashboards establish new patterns of aesthetic engagement with urban objects, resources, or activities. They can invite and even force attention towards something while distracting it from something else. In so doing, technologies are also generating specific hierarchies of worth. They signal that some elements are more important than others in the urban system, and warn that what happens around them is going to be scrutinised and assessed. As a result, the engagement with such urban elements becomes normative, inscribed in a moral regime that, as seen earlier in this section, prescribes new modalities of citizen engagement and activates processes of subjectivation. Yet, while remodulating human attention, digital technologies are also *attentive* to certain things or situations. Tests signal that situations which previously might have gone unnoticed (such as the number of people concentrated in a certain area, or the daily amount of water consumption) have become political issues, if not emergencies. In other words, tests mark the current priorities of the urban agenda: where there are tests, there is also government. In this sense, smart tests produce new maps of power and political goals in the city. Moreover, the technologies reviewed in this chapter are essentially defined by their monitoring functions: drones, water meters, and dashboards detect, measure, and quantify urban experiences. If data collection, measurement, and quantification have always been, to some extent, part of urban governance, smart technologies bring these techniques to an unprecedented level of pervasiveness and persistence. In other words, as it becomes clear that being in the smart city means being under constant scrutiny, quantification becomes normalised as the primary urban rationality and as a standard form of interaction with urban resources, spaces, and people. Politically, this translates into the marginalisation of other methods of approaching urban problems in favour of practices of counting and scoring (Mattern, 2021). As a result, complex problems, such as social vulnerability and resource scarcity are flattened into the presumed objectivity of patterns and risk profiles (O'Neill, 2016; Eubanks, 2018).

To wrap up, this chapter has shown how the testing of smart technologies has effects beyond their immediate functional outcomes. By cultivating forms of smart citizenship, reconfiguring aesthetic regimes, and introducing or disseminating technologies of monitoring, smart tests make the city amenable to quantification and algorithmic management. Tests also prefigure a specific vision of the urban future: one in which the city is governed speculatively, by modelling and preempting the unfolding of events. This form of governance, and its political implications, will be the object of the next chapter.

References

Bulkeley, H., & Castán Broto, V. (2013). Government by experiment? Global cities and the governing of climate change. *Transactions of the Institute of British Geographers, 38*(3), 361–375. https://doi.org/10.1111/j.1475-5661.2012.00535.x

Bulkeley, H., Marvin, S., Palgan, Y. V. (Eds.). (2019). *Urban living labs: Experimenting with city futures.* Routledge.

Case study: How SAP runs Cape Town. (2013, May 21). *Computer Weekly.* https://www.computerweekly.com/news/2240182802/Case-study-How-SAP-runs-Cape-Town

Easterling, K. (2014). *Extrastatecraft: The power of infrastructure space.* Verso Books.

Eubanks, V. (2018). *Automating inequality: How high–tech tools profile, police, and punish the poor.* St. Martin's Press.

Gabrys, J. (2016). *Program earth: Environmental sensing technology and the making of a computational planet.* University of Minnesota Press.

Keating, T. P. (2024). Techno-genesis: Reconceptualising geography's technology from ontology to ontogenesis. *Progress in Human Geography, 48*(1), 49–65. https://doi.org/10.1177/03091325231209020

Kesowa, T. (2021). From re-active to pro-active governance (Project Report). https://kesowa.in/blog-case-studies-whitepapers-and-more

Halpern, O., LeCavalier, J., Calvillo, N., & Pietsch, W. (2013). Test-Bed urbanism. *Public Culture, 25*(2 70), 272–306. https://doi.org/10.1215/08992363-2020602

Howlett, D. (2013). ERP: SAP's journey in Cape Town. [Video Interview]. *Diginomica.* https://diginomica.com/erp-sap-journey-cape-town

Interview 11. (December 2016). MK, IT consultant, Cape Town [in person].

Interview 12. (May 2015). DB, City manager, New Town [in person].

Interview 13. (March 2018). DB, City manager, New Town [Online].

Interview 14. (December 2021). DB, City manager, New Town [Online].

Interview 15. (June 2015). Smart City Consultant A, New Town Kolkata. [in person].

Interview 16. (June 2018). Smart City Consultant A. [Online].

Interview 17. (March 2023). Smart City Consultant A. [Online].

Interview 18. (June 2015). Smart City Consultant B, New Town Kolkata. [in person].

Interview 19. (March 2023). Smart City Consultant B. [online].

Interview 20. (February 2019). FK, IT and management analyst, Cape Town. [online].

Leszczynski, A. (2015). Spatial media/tion. *Progress in Human Geography*, *39*(6), 729–751. https://doi.org/10.1177/0309132514558443

Lockdown: Drone vigil on New Town markets, streets. (2020, May 8). *The Telegraph India*. https://www.telegraphindia.com/west-bengal/calcutta/lockdown-drone-vigil-on-new-town-markets-streets/cid/1771359

Marres, N., & Stark, D. (2020). Put to the test: For a new sociology of testing. *The British Journal of Sociology*, *71*(3), 423–443. https://doi.org/10.1111/1468-4446.12746

Matikinca, P., Ziervogel, G., Enqvist, J. P. (2020). Drought response impacts on household water use practices in Cape Town, South Africa. *Water Policy*, *22*(3), 483–500. https://doi.org/10.2166/wp.2020.169

Mattern, S. (2021). *A city is not a computer: Other urban intelligences*. Princeton University Press. https://doi.org/10.2307/j.ctv1h9dgtj

Millington, N., & Scheba, S. (2021). Day Zero and the infrastructures of climate change: Water governance, inequality, and infrastructural politics in Cape Town's water crisis. *International Journal of Urban and Regional Research*, *45*(1), 116–132. https://doi.org/10.1111/1468-2427.12899

New Town Green City. (2022). *Application of drones in New Town*. https://www.newtowngreencity.in/wp-content/uploads/2022/11/Application-of-Drones-in-New-Town-1.pdf

O'Neill, C. (2016). *Weapons of Math destruction*. Crown Books

Rancière, J. (2004). *The politics of aesthetics: The distribution of the sensible* (G. Rockhill, Trans.). Continuum.

von Schnitzler, A. (2008). Citizenship prepaid: Water, calculability, and techno-politics in South Africa. *Journal of Southern African Studies*, *34*(4), 899–917. https://doi.org/10.1080/03057070802456821

Vanolo, A. (2014). Smartmentality: The smart city as disciplinary strategy. *Urban Studies*, *51*(5), 883–898. https://doi.org/10.1177/0042098013494427

Wright, C., Primo, N., Delbridge, V., & Fortuin, K. (2023). *Data and research as key enablers of city outcomes*: A case study of the City of Cape Town (2000–2022). International Growth Centre. https://www.theigc.org/sites/default/files/2023-01/Wright%20et%20al%20Case%20Study%20January%202023_0.pdf

CHAPTER 4

Futures and Failures: How Speculative Algorithms (Try to) Run the City

In November 2016, the City of Cape Town launched the Emergency Policing and Incident Command (EPIC), a platform that integrates emergency and security services into a single programme for command and control. Powered by SAP High-Performance Analytics Appliance (HANA), EPIC promises to improve efficiency and preparedness in security responses, and to optimise the city's resources, through real-time monitoring and the modelling of future risks (Buckle, 2017). The EPIC platform stems from the more than decennial implementation of the ERP system for the management of the city's business processes examined in the previous chapter. By integrating information from all city departments into a single database accessible to security operators, EPIC is designed not only to make emergency response quicker and more effective, but also to anticipate potential incidents through algorithmic predictions. Around the same time in New Town Kolkata, Xpresso, a proprietary Natural Language Processing software developed by Indian company Abzooba, was being tested to process social media data from local residents for security purposes (Smart City Proposal Annexures, n.d., p. 131). Originally developed to help companies analyse customer feedback, Xpresso was customised to enable urban authorities exploit large volumes of unstructured data, such as social media content, to gain, in the words of its developers, a 'structured birds-eye view about different aspects (Police, Transportation, Healthcare, Water, Road, etc.) of city and

© The Author(s), under exclusive license to Springer Nature   83
Switzerland AG 2025
I. Antenucci, *Future-proofed*,
https://doi.org/10.1007/978-3-031-86429-2_4

citizen sentiment (positive, negative, neutral) about each of these aspects' (n.d, p. 131). The application runs cognitive bots that are able to translate 'text into context', to understand the nuances of human expression, and to classify the intentions of those who write. By performing sentiment analysis, Xpresso is supposed to provide early warnings for citizens' discontent, mounting protests, and potential incidents or unrest.

Here, the EPIC and Xpresso platforms are starting points to reflect on the strategies of urban government that emerge from the implementation of computing infrastructures. After exploring narratives and testing in the previous chapters, this one delves into yet another facet of speculative urbanism, linked to the operational logics of security platforms. The computing technologies deployed for urban security are often read though the categories of surveillance or dataveillance (Lyon, 2018; Murakami Wood & McKinnon, 2019); but those, I argue, are only partially adequate. Drawing on research across different disciplines, from computer science, to critical data studies and security studies, I rather examine the ways in which algorithms shape specific forms of knowledge and action, which are speculative in that they seek not only to *predict*, but also to *produce* distinct futures at the same time. The modelling techniques that are at the core of predictive analytics and automated decisions define a specific relation between security, time, and actions, which involves the future as well as the present. As Marieke de Goede argues (2012) in her study of the prosecution of terrorist money, security is made speculative by the hypothetical, self-referential, and politically charged nature of the algorithmic calculations on which security decisions are based. At the same time, algorithmic security is speculative, as it seeks to make the indefinite configurations of future events available for action in the present. Thus, speculative security combines the two key elements of anticipation—the attempt to calculate future scenarios— and investment, making the future operable in the present. For Jennifer Gabrys (2016), in the experimentation and implementation of new technologies, speculation is a practice that makes the future present by shaping the modalities in which cities are lived and evolve. Speculation is simultaneously a calculative logic performed by algorithms and a practice through which infrastructure and cities are created and governed. Placing the focus on the productive character of algorithms, Agnieszka Leszczyński (2016) describes algorithmic modelling as *future-ing* practices that embed extant urban inequalities and 'project them forward in time and space' (Leszczyński, 2016, p. 1693). Algorithmic future-ing can be situated within the anticipatory turn in contemporary forms of security and governmentality (Anderson, 2010; Amoore, 2011, 2013) that operates through speculative calculations (Aradau, 2015; De Goede et al., 2014). Speculative here designates the intrinsic logic of analytics, which are 'designed to anticipate and shape the unfolding of possibilities, particularly those around social deviance, risk and unrest' (Leszczyński, 2016, p. 1692).

In looking at the ways in which EPIC and Xpresso process urban data and make security decisions, I consider two principal aspects. First, I point out the ways in which algorithmic decisions about urban security are affected by, and affect in turn, situated conditions of socio-spatial inequality and racialised discrimination. The political risks attached to the implementation of algorithmic systems for urban governance have not gone unnoticed. Stephen Graham (2005) made clear, almost two decades ago, how software *sorts* the city and (re)configures socio-spatial and power relations in ways that are prone to discrimination. As data-driven systems take over urban governance, the complexity of urban life is reduced to a (non)matter of computational problems (Mattern, 2013), and becomes standardised through software parameters (McNeill, 2015). Politics is more and more hollowed out by a techno-solutionist approach, whereby each and every socio-political issue can be fixed, or even removed, through yet another software or device (Morozov, 2013). In this chapter, I situate the future-ing practices of security platforms into a broader operational context and examine how situated patterns of socio-spatial inequality factor in the calculations and decisions of the platform. Drawing on critical literature, I then take a closer look at the specific algorithmic techniques at work in EPIC and Xpresso, showing how they rearrange and speculate across urban data. I argue that these speculative techniques have political relevance, in that they produce distinct configurations of knowledge and action—the performance analytics, the risk model—which have the power to affect and mould the trajectories of urban futures.

'Security Goes EPIC in Cape Town'

EPIC incorporates seven departments—metro police, law enforcement, traffic services, emergency services, fire and rescue, disaster management, and the special investigations unit—into a single command and control platform. At the time of this research, authorities were also aiming to include neighbourhood watches, citizen apps, and contraventions in the system (Buckle, 2017). Developed by SAP, in partnership with the South African consulting firm EOH, the platform runs on High-Performance Analytics Appliance (HANA), SAP's signature platform for data management. HANA was originally developed to improve SAP ERP applications for large companies. It integrates in-memory database services, analytics processing, and application development, and is highly flexible and customisable. Within the custom-built EPIC platform, HANA supports SAP's Investigative Case Management, a package that has been specifically created for the public security sector. It features analytics, designed to unearth large and complex patterns of 'crime' across large volumes of data, and modules from EOH, such as their Computer Aided Dispatch with GIS system and their Emergency and Incident Management Solution.

HANA's Business Intelligence comprises several types of analytics, which can be launched simultaneously on a single dataset. The core of the platform's intelligence lies in its machine learning predictive analytics, which consist of SAP's proprietary algorithms. These provide a number of functions, including classification, regression, clustering, time series, key influencers, recommendations, and link analysis. EPIC's analytics are fed data from two main sources: one is a distributed apparatus of sensing devices, such as GPS trackers, cameras, mobile apps, fire detectors, etc., and which connect the human and non-human components of the emergency services, from ambulances to smoke sensors, from policemen to fire hydrants; the other one consists of databases from all city departments, which might be used to improve emergency responses as well as to calculate future risks. For example, as former city's CIO André Steltzner explains in an interview: 'When the fireman has to run into the building our land use management system needs to be able to render the building plan and where the LP (*liquefied petroleum, a/n*) gas cylinders are onto his handheld device so in route to to the fire (…) the commander must be able to actually pull information which will come from other non-emergency related activities like approving a business building plan into his console so that he can guide his his troops accordingly. it's that kind of future that that we see (…) it has to be real time, we can't wait you know a few minutes while we download an image when a building is burning' (Howlett, 2013).

In the central command and control room, dashboards and interactive maps display real-time data, such as livestream images of the city, and the position of incidents and response units (SAP News, 2017; Smith & Mortimer, 2017). This is 'the big picture'; the supposedly holistic view over the city's security status. Officers in the control room are able to contact, deploy, and redirect resources, simply by moving icons on the displays. Policemen, firefighters, medical staff, and other emergency workers are provided with vehicle computers and mobile apps that track their movements, and which allow them to upload content, such as pictures and videos, while giving them access to relevant incident-related information (SAP News, 2017; Smith & Mortimer, 2017).

Over the past two decades or so, platforms for the management of emergencies, traffic, and urban services, have become a landmark of smart city projects across the globe. The Operation Centre of Rio de Janeiro, developed by IBM and launched for the Olympic Games in 2016, has been described as a global template for a new form of urban governmentality shaped by corporate standards, pivoted around digital infrastructures, and embracing a logic of perpetual emergency (Marvin et al., 2015, p. 15). In his study on Rio's Operation Centre, Donald McNeill (2015) shows how the smart dashboard mobilises specific techniques of visualisation—introspection, synopsis, supervision/inspection, and foresight—which have been instrumental for urban government over the past two centuries. As city dashboards proliferate—from Baltimore and Chicago, to London, Dublin, and Singapore—Shannon Mattern (2013) observes that these operate an ontological reduction of cities to widgets, as the complexity of the elements and relations that make up the urban environments are forced into mathematical representations and operational tools. In his study of SAP HANA executive dashboards—on which EPIC's dashboard is modelled—Armin Beverungen (2019) notes that HANA is presented as a single source of truth, where truth coincides with data and algorithmic analysis, and human decision-making is subsumed into machine logic and computational procedures.

EPIC, however, is neither a holistic operation centre, like the COR of Rio de Janeiro, nor it is merely an urban dashboard for data visualisation. It is a custom-built command and control platform for emergency and security management where the data collected are operationalised through distinct rationalities and practices. Not only does EPIC collect and visualise urban data, it also generates decisions and interventions about the city. The platform's analytics are designed to create 'predictions' about future incidents and crimes, to indicate the appropriate procedure for each event, and to optimise the allocation of resources. In this sense,

EPIC is a future-ing apparatus, in that it incessantly seeks to anticipate and shape future possibilities. This largely happens through the calculation of Key Performance Indicators (KPIs), which monitor and assess the provision of emergency and security services. In the control room, the screens show maps of the city in which the exact position of each of the vehicles deployed—ambulances, police patrols, fire brigades' trucks—and of each operator on duty, is tracked and monitored incessantly. The maps also visualise real-time updates about traffic jams, roadblocks, and signals and locates emergency cases, such as a car accident or a fire. Operators in the control room are able to dispatch vehicles and workers to the emergency site by dragging icons on the map. The dragging instantly results in an alert on the workers' smartphone or tablet, featuring information about the accident and the fastest route to get there. The interface of EPIC features a set of tools, icons, and elements of data visualisation— for example, speedometers that indicate if a certain operation is 'on target' or 'over target'—that are common to software specifically designed for the logistics industry. But beyond the visual layer, the affinities extend to other core components of the programmes. Like logistics drivers or warehouse workers, the performances of emergency workers in Cape Town, and of the security supply chain as a whole, are subject to algorithmic KPIs. During their shifts, and especially during emergency interventions, emergency respondents—which include police officers, paramedics, and firefighters—are incessantly monitored. Their activities are measured through parameters such as the time it takes them to reach a certain destination, how long it takes for an accident to be resolved, the number of units involved, and the overall cost of the intervention. The stated purpose of the application of KPIs is to optimise emergency response, improve effectiveness, and better allocate resources. This means that the performances of security workers and of the security supply chain as a whole may affect the organisation of shifts and tasks, the budget assigned to each department, the structure of the chain of command and possibly other normative measures. Since KPIs are calculated via machine learning, the good or bad performance of individual workers or units is immediately embedded into an automated memory that models future working hours, salaries, procedures, and workplace relations.

Studies in the field of logistics have drawn attention to the violence that is embedded in KPIs and parameters for optimisation in the management of labour. The incessant monitoring and measuring of performances, and the pressure to comply with standards of efficiency and cost-effectiveness translate into a heavy toll on the bodies and minds of workers, who find themselves under the perpetual threat of punishment and layoffs (Cowen, 2014; Cuppini et al., 2015; Rossiter, 2016). The specific criteria through which EPIC's algorithms calculate KPIs and model future decisions remain hidden and inaccessible to public scrutiny or, in my case, to research. It is therefore difficult to assess the exact impact that the algorithmic management of the supply chain of security is having on workers' conditions, and how factors such as gender, colour, or ethnicity are taken into account into the calculation of KPIs. Yet those have effects not only on the working conditions of emergency respondents, but also on the urban environment in a broader sense. KPIs classify not only the performance of workers, but also the quality of urban emergencies. Algorithms assign different levels of priority and generate risk alerts on different time ranges, from real-time to broader intervals. Priority and risk models indicate in which areas of the city and on which types of incidents security services should focus their attention, and guide the spatial distribution of patrols, paramedics, and fire brigades across specific neighbourhoods. Here, the logistical management of urban security meets the preemptive strategies of the predictive policing software, such as Hunchlab and Predpol, which have been employed in recent years in several cities in the US, including Philadelphia, Chicago, St. Louis, Santa Cruz, and New Orleans (Benbouzid, 2019; Chammah & Hansen, 2016). One of the business requirements that guided the creation of EPIC was indeed to 'drive proactive policing as opposed to reactive (…) to gain insights into trends and what if Capability to aid in proactive policing based on past offences in a particular local or area', that is, to identify crime hotspots in the city in collaboration with private security (Smith & Mortimer, 2017).

Platforms like Hunchlab and Predpol use analytics to 'predict'—in fact, to *model*—when and where a crime will occur, combining police data with other datasets such as maps and temporal data (school holidays, social events, weather, etc.). They generate risk maps that show boxes in the areas of the city where a crime is predicted to occur within a given timeframe. They have also been accused to target disproportionately black and hispanic communities, therefore reinforcing long-standing patterns of racial abuse. The software developers deny the accusations and claim that their products are race-blind, as analytics do not compute individual backgrounds, but geographical areas and their crime history. Yet urban history and geography are far from neutral, especially in highly segregated North American cities, where urban areas are often proxies for race and class (O'

Neill, 2016, p. 76). This is also true for Cape Town, where the apartheid laws are in the recent past, while de facto segregation persists, along with mistrust and tensions between poor black communities and the police. For example, Cape Town's townships such as Khayelitsha regularly feature in the top ranks of criminal statistics. Township residents and activists, such as the Social Justice Coalition, have long lamented a twofold discrimination from law enforcement: on one hand, the lack of protection against serious crimes in their communities (Commission of Inquiry, 2014); on the other, the systematic targeting and violence against black people, be them homeless, protestors, or just passers-by, especially when found in white(r) and wealthy areas of the city (Samara, 2011). In such a context, it is fair to ask whether a system of crime prediction that is based on geo-historical crime records might be able to address the demands of black communities for non-racist and more equitable forms of policing and security provision. By design, the EPIC platform looks rather likely to reproduce and even reinforce patterns of racial discrimination and abuse. Moreover, as Cathy O'Neill notes (2016), predictive policing systems are designed to target street crime only, and remain blind to so-called 'white collar' crime—infractions, corruption, and fraud committed in the financial and political circles. EPIC too, seems to share this blind spot: its operational parameters are based on street policing and activities such as patrolling, emergency calls, and security cameras. None of those is able to monitor or investigate other types of 'silent' violations happening beyond close doors. Hence, the politics of parameters performed by these platforms shows a tendency to crystallise, and 'techwash' long settled politics of race and class into a supposed neutrality and mathematical objectivity (Benjamin, 2019).

LISTENING TO THE VOICE OF CITIZENS?

As Xpresso's cognitive bots churn data from Facebook and other social media posts, a dashboard displays specific alerts for different kind of risks—from environmental hazards to crime or political protests—which are supposed to enable authorities to 'drill down', examine content in detail, and take suitable 'corrective measures' (Smart City Proposal Annexures, n.d., p. 131) based on context and contingencies. Xpresso had been tested before in an unspecified South Asian city, generating several 'benefits', including the capability to measure public opinion, make more informed decisions on new policies, and better evaluate existing policies.

It made it possible to 'safeguard the country's reputation' by monitoring social media conversations and how these might affect overseas investors and tourists' opinions of the country. It anticipated outbreaks of disease, by correlating searches for specific symptoms, and improved disaster response by understanding the situation on the ground. It prevented and mitigated potential crises through 'active listening'. And finally, it 'transform [ed the] security clearance process' by leveraging social media data for 'national security, background investigations, program integrity, insider threat detection, and more' (Abzooba, n.d).

Agnieszka Leszczynski (2016) analyses a similar application, British sentiment analytics' engine EMOTIVE (Extracting the Meaning of Terse Information in a Geo–Visualisation of Emotion). Developed after the protests and riots in the summer of 2011 in the UK, where mobile social networks played a key role, EMOTIVE generates 'mood maps' of UK cities and serves them to security agencies, to prevent 'potentially harmful events' (EMOTIVE, n.d.). Like EMOTIVE, Xpresso is also designed to generate early warnings for generic undesired situations, by sorting social media posts into different types of emotion—anger, disgust, fear, joy, sadness, and surprise—and expressions—advocacy, complaint, suggestion, and opinion, and by allegedly detecting the intentions of the authors. But more significantly, Leszczynski's analysis of EMOTIVE makes clear how the use of this kind of software in context is always politically charged. EMOTIVE seeks to securitise the city against social unrest and political protests, 'even where such risks exist only in speculative form as codi-fied urban derivatives' (2016, p. 1700). Despite claims of data neutrality and objectivity, the software in fact reinforces a political agenda—protests need to be stopped from spreading—as well as classist and racist urban *topoi*, such as assuming that riots typically happen in neighbourhoods inhabited by specific ethnic and religious groups. This angle is relevant to the testing of Xpresso in New Town as well. Similarly to EMOTIVE, the purpose of the software is to enable urban authorities to act before threats materialise, be they social protests, outbreaks of disease, or traffic jams. Yet such preemptive initiatives are far from neutral, and are actu-ally infused with socio-political assumptions and speculations. Take this example, made by a city official: risk models from Xpresso warned New Town authorities that incidents were likely to happen in a middle-class apartment complex. It turned out that a group of residents were insis-tently complaining on social media about their street being unsafe because of the presence of men 'loitering day and night'. The police intervened quickly, making sure that the 'loitering' would stop 'before any incident or crime happened' (Interview 13, 2018). Like 'encroachment' (as seen in previous chapters) 'loitering' is another term that recurs in Indian public discourses to stigmatise the presence of low-income, lower-caste people, especially men, in urban public spaces (Phadke et al., 2011). Here, Xpresso generated a risk alert speculating on middle-class anxieties, whereby the actual possibility of crime was inferred from socio-spatial tensions. The example also reveals a normative bias in urban authorities, whereby the safety concerns and social media complaints of middle-class residents matter much more than the right to public space of the poor, which is reflected in, and enhanced by, machine learning models.

Chances are that while I am writing this book, an updated version of Xpresso is regularly processing social media posts in New Town Kolkata. Or maybe not. What happened exactly between Xpresso and New Town authorities after the first phase of testing remains unclear. The results of the test and decisions around the adoption of platforms for social media monitoring were never disclosed or discussed in any public form. Silence is itself an argument here, pointing to the asymmetries of knowledge and power that more and more inform the deployment of technologies in government fields, with serious implications for democratic politics (O'Neill, 2016). More specifically to the context, the blackboxing of the Xpresso test resonates with other discriminatory practices in the planning and making of New Town smart city (Gosh & Arora, 2021). Opacity notwithstanding, following Marres and Stark's remark that 'More important than the 'test results' is *what results from the test*' (2020, p. 430), it is possible to follow the traces that Xpresso left in narratives and strategies of urban governance. For government officials, the Xpresso test has marked a milestone in the making of the smart city, ushering a novel approach to urban government. There is a before and after the Xpresso test: before, local authorities lament a lack of knowledge about urban 'moods' and potentially mounting discontent. They were 'always one step behind' regarding what was perceived as an issue among citizens, and could only react once complaints ('grievances', in New Town's bureaucratic language) or even protests had manifested. Xpresso provided them with a platform for acting proactively, for identifying and anticipating potential risks (Interview 13, 2018). The 'before' and 'after' narrative appears, however, as a rhetorical construction that borrows much of its content from smart city propaganda. Stereotypes on data and algorithms as the 'cure' for 'sick' cities, which can be found in advertising material produced by consultants and commercial providers, have seeped undisputed into the language of policymakers. In line with the comments made by government officials, for the consultants the value of this technology lies essentially in its anticipatory power. Regardless of the specific issues at stake, they believe that incidents, crimes, as well as public protests and confrontations, are 'a waste of time and resources for everyone', which could be saved instead by proacting (Interviews 17 & 19, 2023). Acting upon 'security issues', whatever those might be, whether real or perceived, before any incident happens not only improves the safety of the urban environment, but also helps urban authorities manage their resources more efficiently. Furthermore, social media analyses might help urban authorities 'learn' from citizens, not only about what they perceive as risks and concerns, but also about what kind of strategies they spontaneously adopt to deal with those. In so doing, the consultants believe that New Town authorities might discover and validate some informal 'good practices', which could be incorporated to some degree into formal policies. This would ultimately enhance the participation of citizens in urban governance, making them feel 'heard and involved', thus defusing time-consuming events such as 'grievances, bad publicity, or protests' (Interview 17). These comments reflect a techno-solutionist approach towards governance, which prioritises efficient problem-solving (or the perception of) at the expense of political engagement with urban matters. Public confrontations and unrest are framed as intrinsically negative, something to be neutralised before it even starts. At the same time, participation in urban governance is reconfigured as a one-way, vertical process of data extraction and assessment, whereby selected citizens' practices are potentially assimilated.

According to its developers, Xpresso is designed to 'listen to the voice of citizens' (Abzooba, n.d.). This seemingly neutral or even benign task is, in fact, controversial and strongly political, and even more so in a context like New Town. Who is really being listened to through social media monitoring, and who counts as a citizen in the 'smart' city? My conversations with city officials and consultants suggest that there are clear socio-economic perimeters around the social media profiles monitored (Interview 6, 2016). In other words, Xpresso seems to have been largely employed to survey middle-class users, concerned with urban safety and beautification, hardly including other groups of urban dwellers, such as people living in informal settlements. If the 'participatory' processes of 'smart' city planning systematically leave out poorer citizens and marginal communities (Gosh & Arora, 2021), with Xpresso we can observe how the deployment of technologies for social media monitoring reflects a vision of urban citizenship that excludes many. Not only is access to digital technologies filtered along the lines of class and social position, but computing infrastructures also select and hierarchise objects of attention within the urban environment. Indeed, the case of Xpresso in New Town does not entirely fit into the surveillance paradigm that commonly underpins critiques of this kind of application. Usual concerns about the extraction and manipulation of personal data certainly apply to those citizens who are monitored on social media. At the same time, a large part of New Town's residents is not subject to these forms of surveillance because their socio-economic position excludes them from social media monitoring in the first place. Ned Rossiter (2016) uses the term 'post-population' to describe those who escape algorithmic attention on their labour or social life, but whose anonymity comes at the cost of extreme precariousness and vulnerable conditions, such as the dispossessed farmers and slum dwellers of Rajarhat. Interestingly, the same groups of people who are the objects of security in the drone test, are ignored and silenced by design in the Xpresso test. Indeed, unlike EMOTIVE, which is used to monitor and prevent unrest from 'dangerous' parts of the city, the testing of Xpresso seems to focus on the most 'valuable' and 'desired' groups of residents, on validating their concerns, and on managing urban security based on their needs and anxieties. In this sense, Xpresso accelerates the hierarchisation of public space—both online and offline—along lines of class and community. It also shifts the logic of urban government towards techniques of anticipation and preemption, which, at least in the view of 'smart' city promoters, are meant to bypass and replace democratic engagement.

SURVEILLANCE, DATAVEILLANCE, AND BEYOND

The proliferation of infrastructures devoted to data sourcing, identification, and profiling throughout cities has been largely registered as a phenomenon of surveillance and dataveillance (Kitchin, 2014; Tufekci, 2014). Smart cities, David Lyon (2018) argues, foster the normalisation of surveillance. Metaphors such as "the new panopticon" (McMullan, 2015) or "the big brother city" (King, 2016) have been used in the media to describe cities that are monitored from dashboards, where data about anyone and anything are tracked all the time, and where anonymity becomes impossible. Such visions of total surveillance or dataveillance may be desirable for some purveyors of authoritarianism. Yet, and fortunately, there is no evidence that is happening so far. This is not to dismiss the issue of surveillance altogether, or the risks attached to computing infrastructures. But rather than cultivating paranoia about what these technologies are not, at least so far, doing, we should be attentive to what exactly they are doing. Sensors and algorithms do not really see, hear, or track everything and everybody at the same time or in the same way. Quite the opposite, examples like EPIC and Abzooba indicate that computing infrastructures select and hierarchise objects of attention within the urban environment along the lines of class and race.

Indeed, the panopticon/big brother paradigms have been challenged within and beyond surveillance studies for some time already. More than three decades ago, in his book *War in the Age of Intelligent Machines* (1991), philosopher Manuel De Landa observed how surveillance was becoming increasingly distributed and decentralised: 'Instead of positioning some human bodies around a central sensor, a multiplicity of sensors is deployed around all bodies: its antenna farms, spy satellites and cable-traffic intercepts feed into its computers all the information that can be gathered. This is then processed through a series of "filters" or key-word watch lists. The Panspectron does not merely select certain bodies and certain (visual) data about them. Rather, it compiles information about all at the same time, using computers to select the segments of data relevant to its surveillance tasks' (DeLanda, 1991, p. 206).

David Murakami Wood (2013) expanded on Bruno Latour's (2005) concept of 'oligoptic' surveillance, which is intense but partial rather than totalising as in the panopticon, to define systems of surveillance that are broad and unfocused. Smart urban projects can make cities oligoptic (Murakami Wood & McKinnon, 2019) insofar as there is no total view or necessary points of view that add up. Rather, some elements of the urban collective or assemblage (people, places, things, itineraries, feelings, etc.) are subject to intense surveillance, whereas for other elements it is much less so and even not at all (Murakami Wood & McKinnon, 2019, p. 180). In recent years, surveillance has been defined not only as a danger or degeneration but also as a constitutive aspect of the data mining systems that more and more organise every aspect of life. David Lyon (2018) argues that a surveillance culture has emerged, based on the engagement and participation of both the surveillance actors and the surveillance subjects. Surveillance has become user-generated and horizontal; it is performed through social media and distributed throughout everyday life. Since the development of ubiquitous IT infrastructures, Lyon writes, surveillance has become a way of life and a mode of societal organisation, from credit ratings and no-fly lists, to self-monitoring through wearables and social media engagement. Surveillance today is, literally, part of our furniture, as smart meters, smartphones, and all sorts of smart devices log our location, measure our activities, and register our "likes" and our contacts (Lyon, 2018, p. 84). In literature, surveillance and dataveillance are often treated as a conceptual and practical continuum. Dataveillance is defined as ubiquitous surveillance through meta(data) (Raley, 2013). In this sense, it seems to be mere technological evolution of surveillance in the age of big data, from which it differs only in terms of scale and efficiency. This is intuitively and loosely true, as key features of surveillance, such as monitoring and scrutinising, are also common to dataveillance. However, as José Van Dijck (2014) notes, dataveillance differs from surveillance in at least one important aspect: whereas surveillance presumes monitoring for specific purposes, dataveillance entails the continuous tracking of (meta)data for unstated purposes. It does not limit itself to scrutinising individuals, but infiltrates multiple, dispersed aspects of the social fabric (2014, p. 205), including objects, animals, plants, and natural resources. I believe there is something more to this. Surveillance comes from the French word, *surveiller*, literally, to watch over. The term implies a gaze from above, which is clearly identifiable (even if not visible) as a recognised authority—the eye of the prison guards, of the spy, or Big Brother. The identity of the surveillant might remain unknown (as in the panopticon or with the secret police), but the diagram of power clearly manifests through the practice of surveillance. This does not necessarily happen in the landscape of big data and computing infrastructures.

Unlike surveillance, dataveillance does not only, or primarily, watch from above. It also observes from *beside*, through apparently horizontal connections, such as Facebook friends, Instagram and Twitter followers, Uber rides, and the peer-to-peer architecture in general; and from *within*, as we all take part in the monitoring of ourselves and others by using smartphones, search engines, wearables, IoT devices, etc. In most cases, even if we know that our (meta)data are being collected, analysed, and probably sold on by someone or something, we don't know exactly by whom or what, when, and why. The dozens of terms and conditions we accept every day to navigate the web and to use mobile apps, do not tell us what will actually happen to our personal information. This does not mean, of course, that big data is an anarchic or anomic territory. Obviously, Google and Facebook, national security agencies, and any owner of commercial software have more power over data than the average user. There are norms and regulations, albeit already obsolete the second after they are issued. There are hierarchies and strategies, and roles and procedures, but these are largely obscure, or blackboxed. In essence, even in the presence of a legal framework, the actual diagrams of power that operate through dataveillance remain opaque.

In our time, dataveillance is clearly powerful and expansive, and particularly in smart cities. But it does not fully explain systems such as EPIC and Xpresso or more broadly, of data-driven urban governmentality for two reasons. First, despite the efforts of smart city planners, there may not be a straightforward correlation between the infinite amount of data that is gathered through intelligent infrastructures, social media, etc., and government actions. Data are often dispersed among several different actors (states, municipalities, private companies, academic or non-academic researchers, NGOs, activists, hackers, etc.), all of whom pursue different and often conflicting agendas. As the examples from New Town and Cape Town indicate, a number of commercial players are able to access urban data, and this creates wide zones of opacity as to how data are handled and for which purposes. Urban data can be so immense and fragmented that their potential, in terms of actual, actionable knowledge, remains largely under-exploited. Paradoxically, there may well be so much dataveillance that it makes complete dataveillance impossible. In short, data could be wasted, or perhaps, big data as such is waste, until it is dissected by algorithms and reassembled into forms of actionable information. This is one of the problems that smart city projects are trying to address, by creating integrated control platforms.

Second, even if dataveillance is applied to the fullest extent, and no data is wasted, it still does not make a logic of urban government. Dataveillance is a component of data-driven environments, and disposition of the socio-technical assemblages that we live in. But it does not explicate how decisions are taken or strategies take form. Contrary to the common emphasis on the *big* of big data, Louise Amoore and Volha Piotukh (2015) demand attention on the work of the *little* analytics in contemporary forms of knowledge production and government. What matters is not so much accumulating data, but making them *tractable* for commercial or security decisions, through specific practices of data ingestion, partitioning, and memory. This is exactly what happens in platforms such as EPIC and Xpresso: their work is not merely about monitoring more, but about translating what is monitored into models, such as risk alerts and preemptive decisions. Operators in urban control rooms might be able to do more with less data and sharper analytics, than with more data but not the right algorithmic tools. Dataveillance does not explain new forms of urban government, because it merely keeps its focus on the aspect of watching, while overlooking the productive character of algorithms and the key operations—counting, scraping, skinning, connecting, drawing, and, ultimately, modelling—that translate data into action.

SECURITY SPECULATIONS

Platforms like EPIC and Xpresso do not just watch the city; they make decisions about it. As we have seen in the previous pages, they generate configurations of the future that are full of political meanings and implications. A closer look at the logic and procedures of the algorithms that power them helps us understand how these platforms operate in context and how they contribute to urban government. In SAP HANA— EPIC's software backbone—engineers set the parameters for analysis and provide users—that is, city officials and emergency respondents—with a range of customisable options. For example, users can choose the datasets on which algorithms are trained or which specific algorithmic procedure to use for a specific task. Automated performance-tuning capabilities ensure that models are able to adjust as data changes with time. Users can try out many different scenarios, and 'incorporate any improvement that they discover back into models in real-time. They can also schedule model refreshes, manage models by exception, and deploy scores instantly to use results in applications and real-time analysis' (SAP, 2018). In data streaming analysis, where immense volumes of data are incessantly processed, algorithms identify meaningful patterns, create alerts, generate automated responses, and apply predictive models, in order to anticipate what is coming. They also measure data over time, to unearth historical trends, which in turn feed into decision models and forecasts. Analytics apply KPIs to emergency responses, such as measuring the single interventions of the Fire & Rescue Department against an average response time; or classifying the geographical distribution of different types of incidents.

Algorithmic modelling is key to understanding how security platforms like EPIC and Xpresso operate. Modelling is, by definition, the representation of a phenomenon that cannot be observed or acted upon directly. Modelling practices are informed by existing theories and involve making decisions about which relevant aspects need to be represented, and which can be neglected. Yet the process is much less straightforward than it is usually described. As Michael Weisberg (2013) explained, models stand in relationships of similarity with their targets. In other words, they represent their targets in the real world, by sharing some important features of them. Models are similar to their targets insofar as they do not lack too many of these features nor do they have too many extra features. However, maximum similarity between models and targets is not necessarily a goal that modellers pursue, as they often introduce idealisation into their practice; i.e. they deliberately distort their models for the sake of simplifying or isolating certain components. As is evident from computer science literature (Cormen et al., 2009; Garcìa et al., 2015; Larose & Larose, 2015), modelling is largely a matter of attempts, trials, failures, and corrections. It involves creativity, intuition, and luck as much as it does mathematical knowledge and rigour. As authors frequently remind their readers, the choice of the specific task (association, clustering, regression, etc.) to be undertaken to extract knowledge from data, and of the specific algorithm(s) to be used for that same task, is highly contingent and is determined by a wide range of factors. These can include, for example, the type of datasets available and the level of tolerance of the algorithm to data flaws, such as missing values and noise; the calculative speed of the algorithm compared to the computational power (and, broadly speaking, the money) on which researchers can count; the storage available, and the volume of data required for a given algorithm to perform adequately; the background and specific skills of the professionals involved; and potentially countless other factors linked to hardware, funding, deadlines, personal inclinations, etc. It is for these reasons that Nick Seaver (2014) invites his readers to pay attention, not only to algorithms as computational procedures but also to the algorithmic systems' 'intricate, dynamic arrangements of people and code' (p. 9), through which the formulae come to life and impact the world. Algorithms are trained, tested, and amended, over wide and complex networks of professionals, machine, and algorithmic systems. It is in these networks that ideas are translated into code, and that code, in turn, translates life into models.

In the aftermath of 9/11, security agencies and governments were compelled to focus on 'low-probability, high-impact' events that challenged the forms of risk calculation that had been in use until that time, and to incorporate an increased degree of imagination into their procedures (Amoore, 2013). As Benedict Anderson (2010) writes in a seminal paper on the governance of the future, government in our time is informed by anticipatory action—the logics of preemption, precaution, and preparedness—whose specificity is that it works on undetermined, potential future scenarios. The nature of security practices has thus become *speculative*, as it no longer settles for probabilistic evidence, but increasingly looks for the unknown and the improbable, while trying to draw the multiplicity of possible futures into present decisions. As de Goede, Simon and Hojitnik (2014) note, security is speculative, not because it is imaginative or unreal but because it deploys notions of futurity that parallel the technologies of financial speculation. As in financial speculation, preemption is not as much about predicting the future as it is about acting on multiple potential futures that are rendered actionable (or liquid) in the present (de Goede et al., 2014, p. 13, drawing on Amoore, 2013; Cooper, 2010; de Goede, 2012). This twofold meaning of speculation, fusing hypothesis and capitalisation, is closely linked to the operational logic of modelling that supports security decisions.

The specific algorithms at work in platforms, such as EPIC or Xpresso, are proprietary and secret, as are most of the algorithms in use for commercial or government purposes (O'Neill, 2016; Pasquale, 2015). Nonetheless, it is possible to discuss their operations, as Claudia Aradau and Tobias Blanke (2015) suggest, drawing on the state- of-the-art knowledge, demos, tutorials, user guides, and data science blogs. In order to bridge the gap between the study of the 'outside' of algorithms—their social life and effects—and their 'inside'—code, maths, and concrete applications —Bernhard Rieder (2017) proposes focussing on the algorithmic techniques, or 'the finite set of well-known approaches to information filtering and classification that underpin most running systems' (p. 101). Even if there is no way to know the exact formulae that operate in platforms like EPIC or Xpresso, scrutinising the type of algorithms in use and how they are combined to perform specific tasks can still provide insights into platform operations. For example, the Predictive Analysis Library (PAL) of SAP/HANA suggests nine categories of functions: clustering, classification, association, regression, time series, pre-progressing, statistics, social network analysis, and miscellaneous. (SAP, 2018). Each category comprises several different algorithms, which can be combined to generate the desired models. While the specific procedures in use remain blackboxed, it is still possible, and helpful, to examine their basic rules and logics or, in line with Rieder (2017), the algorithmic techniques they put to work. These include, for example, pre-processing techniques, which clean up and prepare data for analysis. Data needs to be stripped of all those elements that algorithms cannot read, and to be translated into a set of parameters. Computer scientists García and colleagues (2015) identify six principal problems that can emerge with datasets: dirtiness, inaccuracy, fragmentation, different measurement units, missing values, and noise; and the related techniques to fix them: cleaning, transformation, integration, normalisation, missing data imputation, and noise identification. Whereas the notion of data cleaning is often used to describe pre-processing in general and comprises techniques such as noise identification and missing values imputation, it also concerns the 'detection of discrepancies and dirty data (fragments of the original data which do not make sense)' that typically requires human supervision (p. 11). Missing values in datasets—a very frequent problem in data preparation—are often simply ignored, or the incomplete dataset is discarded. This can lead to biased results: 'For example when low income individuals are less likely to report their income level, the resulting mean is biased in favor of higher incomes' (Garcia et al., 2015, p. 63). Alternatively, missing values can be replaced with estimates calculated with statistical methods. What matters here is that the question of how missing values in incomplete data sets are replaced—a very frequent circumstance when dealing with data 'from the real world', like urban data—is still very much a work in progress and remains a topic of debate between scholars and professionals. Decisions about which technique to use depend on a number of contextual factors and assumptions. Yet scholars recognise that each technique for imputing missing values—which is only one among many techniques for data preparation—involves some degree of loss or corruption of the information. This is particularly true when data are not missing randomly, rather their absence is linked to one or more specific reasons, which may remain neglected in the subsequent analysis of data (Baraldi & Enders, 2010; Hughes et al., 2019).

Sampled, smoothed, and normalised, algorithm-ready data do not retain a great deal of the living world they came from. Pre-processing algorithms are a first layer of mediation between so-called 'raw' data and analytics, and help to reframe 'real world' problems into computable terms. Because urban platforms, such as EPIC, promise to deliver deep and accurate insights and a holistic view of the city, it is important to consider the multiplicity of elements that actually make up a city, and in light of the filtering techniques described above, to consider and imagine what might be discarded and with what effect. By selecting what to calculate—and here I am reiterating Shannon Mattern's remarks about urban dashboards (2013)—algorithms make normative decisions about what matters and what doesn't matter in the city and, ultimately, what the city is or is not. Given this, algorithms perform an epistemic and ontological reduction of cities to their data derivatives—models—which begins with pre-processing functions. If a powerful *mythology* of big data, according to which the algorthmic analysis of large data sets would deliver objective and accurate truth (Boyd & Crawford, 2012), widely circulates in policy and academic circles, many have drawn attention to the mystifications and biases that this narrative conceals. To start, there is no inherent connection between data and truth. 'Data has no truth', writes Daniel Rosenberg (2013, p. 37). 'It may be that the data we collect and transmit has no relation to truth or reality whatsoever beyond the reality that data helps us to construct. (…) it is this rhetorical aspect of the term "data" that has made it indispensable'. Data are not facts, but rather a basis for rhetorical arguments. As Lisa Gitelman and Virginia Jackson (2013) make clear, drawing on Bowker (2005), there is no such thing as raw data. Data are neither neutral, nor innocent; they are always inscribed in a set of discursive and material coordinates; they are imagined, selected, presented, and organised. An interpretative framework and, in practice, a set of pre-processing techniques, always prefigures data analysis.

Once data has been prepared—cleaned up, transformed, normalised, and integrated—they are ready to be 'mined': dissected by algorithms in search of meaningful information, from which predictive models can be generated. Clustering, for example, is a key function of HANA'S predictive library, largely employed in unsupervised learning and applied to tasks such as pattern recognition and anomaly detection. Frequently employed in the early stages of data mining as a way of reducing and simplifying information, especially when dealing with large volumes of data, clustering algorithms seek to segment the entire data set into relatively homogeneous subgroups or clusters. Clustering can be done through different mathematical approaches, but all operate under the assumption that all the elements in the same cluster will have more in common with each other than with the elements of another cluster. Classification techniques combine different variables associated with a certain class of objects (the training dataset) to determine further possible associations in new datasets. Well-known examples of these techniques include predicting the credit risk associated with a mortgage application, or whether certain behaviours indicate a potential terrorist threat (Larose & Larose, 2015). Bayesian classifiers such as decision trees, for example, are an influential classification technique that infers the probability of a hypothesis—e.g. that an email is spam—based on existing knowledge. Decision trees seek to decrease the entropy, i.e. the amount of information, generated by each data point. Entropy is a definition of disorder and uncertainty, hence reducing the entropy of a tree node means higher probability and accuracy. Also widely used to make predictions, regression algorithms estimate relationships among variables, i.e. they measure how dependent variables change, when any independent variable, known as a predictor, changes. Association techniques, including algorithms such as a-priori, FP growth, K-optimal rule discovering, and sequential pattern mining, unearth hidden patterns and correlations among sets of items or objects.

As this brief review of data mining techniques indicates, algorithms assemble information through criteria of resemblance and correspondence, and identify patterns based on proximity, imitation, analogy, and sympathy. This, Claudia Aradau (2015) provocatively argues, seems closer to divination than to scientific methods as we know them. Writing about the Bayesian inferences used in many predictive algorithms, Louise Amoore stresses that they work speculatively in unearthing unknown values, which become visible and relevant only when connected to one another in conditional propositions (Amoore, 2013, p. 59). The output of such calculations is not based on facts but on rules of associations. Yet, even if highly speculative, these algorithms are at the same time normative. As Rieder (2017) writes, Bayesian classifiers are 'a form of description that is built, from the ground up, on a prescriptive horizon. We no longer (only) decide based on what we know; we know based on the decision we have to make' (p. 111). Although it is based on a specific form of algorithm, this remark grasps the heuristic tendency of algorithmic systems generally, where the entire chain of knowledge production—from the preparation of data to the training and fine-tuning of models—is led by targets that are grounded in specific interests, be they the selection of new customers, the detection of cancer risk factors, or the identification of suspect criminals.

Natural Language Processing, on which the Xpresso platforms are based, analyses human expressions on social networks. Natural Language Processing can be performed using several techniques, including the aforementioned Bayesian and neural networks. Artificial neural networks are sets of algorithms designed to (loosely) imitate the human brain, and one of the most common machine learning applications. Beyond Natural Language Processing, neural networks can be used to carry out a number of tasks and, therefore, they are transversal to each of the modelling categories described above. Neural networks can be developed within extremely complex structures—as in Deep Learning models—but, in essence, they are made up of a set of interconnected computing nodes (neurons) which receive inputs from both the outside and from other nodes, communicating with each other. They learn through iterative processes, adapting to mistakes—for example, when the network gives a wrong output, or fails to classify the semantic domain of a word, the connections that led to failure are weakened, while those that led to success are reinforced, until the right output is achieved (Fausett, 2014). As Matteo Pasquinelli (2017) observes, neural networks turn information into logic, as 'the logic gates of neural networks compute information in order to affect the way they will compute future information' (2017, p. 7). Proximity and distance, entropy, and feedback loops are instruments of a 'statistics of pure relation' (Bolin & Andersson Schwarz, 2015, p. 2), where information becomes logic, but logic does not permeate information. In other words, there is no necessary relation between the mathematical indicators of proximity or distance within a cluster, entropy in a decision tree, feedback in a neural network, etc., or causality in the 'real' outside world. Even given the fact that algorithms succeed in finding correlations, it does not follow that these correlations are of any consequence outside the model, let alone that they predict future actions.

This close-up on the algorithms at work in EPIC and Xpresso makes clear that what are commonly labelled as predictions are actually suggestions about possible links among sets of data that have been previously filtered to fit into the model, and not the other way round. Models are closed systems, with no logical or practical relationship with the outside except for what is assigned to them by a broader context. In fact, technically speaking, algorithms do not discover patterns (or other models of information) but they fabricate them (Perrotta & Williamson, 2018,

p. 10). Pre-processing and iteration are two clear examples of the procedures through which algorithms are made productive. Under the right conditions, algorithms may use their capabilities not to find, but to create results. As we have seen in the description above, clustering, decision trees, and regression models iterate their calculation several times in order to reduce margins of confusion or error. As David Beer (2018) argues, algorithms are the core product of a rampant and increasingly powerful industry, which aggressively crafts an imaginary wherein data (and) analytics are presented as vital to the future of knowledge, business, and the human condition at large. The affirmation of this rationality, coupled with pervasive marketing strategies and commercial deals, establishes data analytics as the ultimate source of heuristic authority. The gaze on the world—the forms and boundaries of visualisation and sensemaking—that this imaginary dictate is highly performative, as it has the power to shape and manifest the trajectories of the future that it anticipates. 'Clearly data analytics', Beer writes 'are complicit in such imagined futures, meaning that there is a politics to the anticipation they are said to afford. (…) here we see anticipation being ramped up and reactivity being folded into imagined futures' (2018, p. 32).

Beer's remarks bring to the fore the convergence between the two meanings of speculative in the socio-political life of algorithms: the theoretical and the financial. On one hand is the creation of hypothesis and on the other the attempt to make those hypotheses actionable. The purpose of my review of the predictive analytics methods employed by EPIC and Xpresso, was to unearth the speculative logic that is embedded in the algorithmic procedures. The type of knowledge that these algorithms produce is one of mere—albeit automated—statistical induction, where algorithms learn from what they calculate and then turn this into rules for further actions or predictions. As we have seen, these operations require a great deal of preparation—pre-processing algorithms—and fine-tuning attempts, in order to give acceptable results. In other words, despite giving the pretence of superior efficacy, algorithms are not tools that plastically capture data. In fact, it appears to be the other way round: data are groomed and refined so they can fit the algorithms. Pasquinelli (2017, p. 13) points out that algorithms generate hypotheses in the form of inductive inferences, or at best examples of weak abduction (such as medical diagnoses). They are not able to think causally or elaborate dirty data (except, as we will shortly see, for cases of apophenia, i.e. when

106   I. ANTENUCCI

algorithms create patterns from dirty data). These weak forms of speculations are not predictions, but they do offer material for preemption: a selected range of possibilities over which anticipatory action can be taken. However, it does not follow from this that models are purely arbitrary, or that preemption is the only logic around which models are constructed. As Weisberg (2013) suggests, the model-world relationship, that is the degree of actual similarity between them, ultimately depends on how modelling is practised, i.e. how interests, decisions, and practical factors shape the construal of a distinct model. Within the context of this analysis, however, preemption emerges as a key principle for the making of models, grounded in the strategies of urban government that underpin the deployment of platforms such as EPIC and Xpresso.

REALTIMENESS AND PREEMPTION

'The whole idea of things having to be real-time, having to be super fast, was key', says Mehboob Foflonker, Chief Technology Officer of the City of Cape Town, in the EPIC promotional video, while dramatic images of wildfires run in the background (SAP, 2017). If preemption is a key factor of smart city platforms, real-time is the magic word. Emergency services in Cape Town have improved because EPIC is able to gather and share more information in real-time. Urban governance will improve as Xpresso provides real-time insights into citizen's moods and concerns. Dashboards, control rooms, and software increasingly strive to deliver an augmented present. As Rob Kitchin (2017) writes: 'The most critical to the logics and operations of smart urbanism, I propose, concerns "present present" and the ability to be able to monitor, analyse and react in real-time (...) (to achieve) the instantaneous control of space and spatial relations in real-time' (p. 21).

And yet, studies that have critically engaged with realtimeness all conclude that, in fact, there is no such thing. By definition, real-time is the suppression of any latency between the occurrence of an event, and the reporting or recording of it, or between an action and its effects. In his analysis of the early developments of the global internet, Adrian Mackenzie (1997) explains that: 'realtime concerns the rate at which computational processing takes place in relation to the time of lived audio-visual experience. It entails the progressive elimination of any perceptible delay between the time of machine processing and the time of conscious perception' (1997, p. 60). In essence, McKenzie (1997) is saying that real-time is just machine-time; it coincides with computation. More recently, Esther Weltevrede et al. (2014) have drawn attention to the *making* of real-time across digital media; that is, to the multiple ways in which real-time is fabricated across the plethora of digital devices and platforms that we use every day. They conclude that real-time is always device-specific, as it depends on the different computational processes that are used by the different machines and software. Hence, the authors use the notion of *realtimeness* to describe how so-called real-time events are not actually happening in the now, but emerge from the continuous movement of data, the user's engagement, and the filtering of information based on specific algorithmic settings. In sum, 'realtimeness refers to an understanding of time that is embedded in and immanent to platforms, engines and their cultures' (2014, p. 143). Similarly, Rob Kitchin (2017) argues that after closer examination, no so-called real-time system actually works in real-time; there is always some degree of latency. Each system must make choices about the temporal rate of data sampling—every few milliseconds, or every ten seconds, or every five minutes, or any other interval. Furthermore, the timing of data analysis can take place instantly or over time, as can the timing of data sharing with the public, which can be close to immediate or delayed or might never happen. Latencies can also occur, depending on the speed of the network technology that is used—broadband, Wi-Fi, 3G, 4G, Bluetooth, etc. —and also on the system components and architecture. Realtimeness, Kitchin (2017) concludes, is a precarious and fabricated condition; it requires continuous maintenance, patching, and repair, as it is exposed to all sorts of faults, from software crashes to hacking. It is relational, heterogeneous, and contingent.

When it comes to computation, present-present and realtimeness are not only as critical as preemption and modelling of the future, but also inseparable. In fact, the capability to be effective in real-time depends on some degree of anticipation of events. Algorithms that are used for real-time decisions are trained with historical datasets; thus realtimeness is, in practice, a form of quasi-instantaneous preemption. Let us consider the practice of now-casting—the forecasting of now. Now-casting has been used in meteorology for a long time, and more recently it has been used in economics and data analysis in general. Now-casting is defined as 'the prediction of the present, the very near future and the recent past' (Bańbura et al., 2013, p. 2) and 'the exercise of reading, through the lenses of a model, the flow of data releases in real time' (Bańbura et al.,

2013, p. 5). This tool has been used in social media monitoring for quite some time, for instance, to evaluate 'the mood of the nation' from tweets in the UK (Lansdall-Welfare et al., 2012). When the Xpresso engine claims to classify New Town's urban emotions, and to generate early warnings from social media streams of data 'in real-time', or when EPIC's analytics signal an emergency, both tools are practising now-casting—projecting a super short-term model on the present. In synthesis, the logic of modelling that informs urban government platforms compresses past, present, and future into a single mode of calculation. So-called realtimeness is actually a form of extremely fast modelling.

Antoinette Rouvroy and Bernard Stiegler (2016) define preemption as 'an augmented actuality of the possible. (…) This is a specific actuality that takes the form of a vortex aspiring both the past and the future. Everything becomes actual' (2016, p. 15). This definition casts light on how operations of preemption and realtimeness/now-casting deconstruct the boundaries, not only between past, present, and future but also between possibility and reality. The two key criteria of modelling—speculation and actionability—become the foundation for governmental action. Now-casting models quite literally *make* the future *present*, in forms that can be handled immediately and which can potentially codify response protocols for the future. So, now-casting also *performs* the future (Anderson, 2010), insomuch as it shapes the ways in which future possibilities can be understood and attended to.

When Algorithms Fail

Having looked 'inside' EPIC and Xpresso, at the operational logics of their algorithms, let's now consider how these systems relate to the 'world out there': data, time, and the urban environment around them. As seen earlier in this chapter, dirty data, human bias, political context, and socio-spatial factors are some of the reasons why policing models tend to enhance racism and oppressive practices, or why public service algorithms end up persecuting poor communities, instead of providing support. But perhaps, more reasons for these perilous outcomes are entrenched in the very logic of algorithms themselves. In their book *Pattern Discrimination* (2018), Clemens Apprich, Wendy Chun, Florian Cramer, and Hito Steyerl investigate how techniques of pattern recognition perform and reinforce racism, sexism, and classism across social media, search engines and other fields of application. This happens, Chun states, particularly because network science works through homophily, 'the axiom that similarity breeds connection' and that 'love is always love of the same' (2018, p. 60); hence it applies conservative identity politics to data analysis. Homophilic algorithms generate filter bubbles and echo chambers on social media and search engines, which will feed you what you have seen before and (supposedly) want to see again. For example, this explains why white supremacists, on social media, have come to believe they are the majority of people—they live in a filter bubble of southern crosses and communist conspiracies, where Jesus is white and rapists are black. Furthermore, I suggest, homophily is also built into predictive models which assume that parents with a past of domestic violence are likely to abuse their children, hence signal them to social services; or that high crime records in black communities means black people love crime, hence agents are continually directed to black neighbourhoods. Homophily makes biased algorithms powerfully performative, and turns deficient models into discriminating politics.

Two more common flaws of models, which make the tautological, self-referential nature of algorithmic knowledge particularly visible, are overfitting and apophenia. In the case of 'over-fitting', a model learns so much, and so well, from training data that it can only recognise a very specific pattern and is not able to generalise on new data. Facial recognition models that have been trained only with white faces, and which label black faces as 'gorillas'—as in Google's infamous case—are a striking example of overfitting. Conversely, apophenia occurs when models recognise patterns that do not exist or, better, create patterns from dirty data, i.e. datasets that have not been pre-processed. As Hito Steyerl (2018) provocatively suggested, the incorrect targeting of aerial strikes could be examples of apophenic models. Overfitting and apophenia clearly point to the socio-political production of algorithms, where human mistakes and prejudice in the choice of biased training datasets, or in the poor tuning of the model, can produce results that are completely unobjective, and potentially lethal. Overfitting and apophenia also indicate, as Pasquinelli (2017) put it, the 'intrinsic limits in neural computation: they show how neural networks can paranoically spiral around embedded patterns rather than helping to reveal new correlations' (2017, p. 9). In essence, it is the tautological inner rationality of algorithms, and not only human errors in training and supervising them, that make algorithms prone to bias and mistake.

Platforms like EPIC and Xpresso seek to translate the city into the language of predictive algorithms. Although different in size, architecture, and scope, they both are led by preemptive strategies, which seek to model possible future scenarios and to act upon them. They are future-ing dispositifs, concerned with constructing or deconsutructing specific urban futures through a speculative security calculus. Yet, the liability of models to bias, inaccuracy, and even delirium makes their political relevance manifest. Inequalities, exploitation, racism, sexism, frauds, and lies, are often built into the mathematical instruments that transform immense, chaotic volumes of digital traces into knowledge that can be used and monetised. Algorithms are shaped by the cultural environments in which they are created and trained, and similarly, their calculative logics—homophily, tautology, overfitting, and apophenia—are way too prone to normalise, reproduce, and magnify biases and mistakes across correlations, inferences, and decisions. Algorithms are a highly effective, yet self-referential form of knowledge that is commonly presented as intelligence. For algorithms to make sense of the 'world out there', the world needs to be packaged to fit into them, in the form of datasets, samples, bins, and so on.

To conclude, the speculative nature of algorithms, and therefore of algorithm-based security, is a fact of political relevance. It means that algorithms speculate on data, as Aradau (2015) suggested, because they elaborate theoretical constructs rather than producing demonstrable evidence. It also means algorithms speculate insofar as they are designed to extract as much content as possible from data and to return preemptive elements—an actionable version of the future—at any cost. Both these elements have an impact on the ways in which the city is known and governed. Speculation, as enacted by extensive computing systems, actually *makes* the city, because, as Jennifer Gabrys observes, it is 'a practice of constructing particular trajectories of urban practice and inhabitation. Construction occurs here in at least two senses: of being built, and of forming the conditions in which new speculative urbanisms (and modes of withness) may unfold' (2016, p. 244). It is in these continuous practices of production of the future, in the mathematical appropriation of possibilities that new strategies of urban government delineate.

REFERENCES

Abzooba. (n.d.). *Sentiments going viral could have adverse effects on business or governance*. Retrieved January 20, 2019, from https://abzooba.com/resources/case-studies/other-case-studies/sentiments-going-viral-could-have-adverse-effects-on-business-or-governance/

Amoore, L., & Piotukh, V. (2015). Life beyond big data: Governing with little analytics. *Economy and Society*, *44*(3), 341–366. https://doi.org/10.1080/03085147.2015.1043793

Anderson, B. (2010). Preemption, precaution, preparedness: Anticipatory action and future geographies. *Progress in Human Geography*, *34*(6), 777–798.

Amoore, L. (2011). Data derivatives: On the emergence of a security risk calculus for our times. *Theory, Culture & Society*, *28*(6), 24–43.

Amoore, L. (2013). *The politics of possibility: Risk and security beyond probability*. Duke University Press.

Apprich, C., Chun, W. H. K., Cramer, F., & Steyerl, H. (2018). *Pattern discrimination*. University of Minnesota Press.

Aradau, C. (2015). The signature of security: Big data, anticipation, surveillance. *Radical Philosophy*, *191*, 21–28.

Aradau, C., & Blanke, T. (2015). The (big) data-security assemblage: Knowledge and critique. *Big Data & Society*, *2*(2), 1–12. https://doi.org/10.1177/2053951715609066

Bańbura, M., Giannone, D., Modugno, M., & Reichlin, L. (2013). Now–casting and the real-time data flow. In G. Elliott, C. Granger, & A. Timmermann (Eds.), *Handbook of economic forecasting* (Vol. 2, pp. 195–237). Elsevier.

Baraldi, A. N., & Enders, C. K. (2010). An introduction to modern missing data analyses. *Journal of School Psychology*, *48*(1), 5–37.

Benjamin, R. (2019). *Race after technology: Abolitionist tools for the new jim code*. Polity.

Beverungen, A. (2019). Executive dashboard. In T. Beyes, C. Pias, & R. Holt (Eds.), *The Oxford Handbook of media, technology, and organization studies* (pp. 225–237). Oxford University Press.

Buckle, L. (2017, January 22). Meet the crack team behind Cape Town's firefighters. *IOL*. Retrieved February 10, 2018, from https://www.iol.co.za/news/south-africa/western-cape/meet-the-crack-team-behind-cape-towns-firefighters-7555450

Beer, D. (2018). *The data gaze: Capitalism, power and perception*. Sage.

Benbouzid, B. (2019). To predict and to manage: Predictive policing in the United States. *Big Data & Society*. https://doi.org/10.1177/2053951719861703

Bolin, G., & Andersson Schwarz, J. (2015). Heuristics of the algorithm: Big Data, user interpretation and institutional translation. *Big Data & Society*, *2*(2), https://doi:10.1177/2053951715608406.

112   I. ANTENUCCI

Boyd, D., & Crawford, K. (2012). Critical questions for big data: Provocations for a cultural, technological, and scholarly phenomenon. *Information, Communication & Society, 15*(5), 662–679.

Bowker, G. C. (2005). *Memory practices in the sciences*. MIT Press.

Chammah, M., & Hansen, M. (2016). The battle for Chicago: The plan to fix America's most violent city. *The Marshall Project*. Available at https://www.themarshallproject.org

Commission of Inquiry into Allegations of Police Inefficiency and a Breakdown in Relations between SAPS and the Community in Khayelitsha. (2014). *Towards a Safer Khayelitsha*. Available at: https://sjc.org.za/wp-content/uploads/2019/02/Khayelitsha_Commission_Report_WEB_FULL_TEXT_C.pdf

Cooper, M. (2010). Turbulent worlds: Financial markets and environmental crisis. *Theory, Culture & Society, 27*(2–3), 167–190. https://doi.org/10.1177/0263276409358727

Cormen, T. H., Leiserson, C. E., Rivest, R. L., & Stein, C. (2009). *Introduction to algorithms* (3rd ed.). MIT Press.

Cowen, D. (2014). *The deadly life of logistics: Mapping violence in global trade*. University of Minnesota Press.

Cuppini, N., Frapporti, M., & Pirone, M. (2015). Logistics struggles in the po valley: Territorial transformations and processes of antagonistic subjectivation. *South Atlantic Quarterly, 114*(1), 119–134.

de Goede, M. (2012). *Speculative security: The politics of pursuing terrorist monies*. University of Minnesota Press.

De Goede, M., Simon, S., & Hoijtink, M. (2014). Performing preemption. *Security Dialogue, 45*(5), 411–422.

De Landa, M. (1991). *War in the age of intelligent machines*. Zone Books.

Fausett, L. V. (2014). *Fundamentals of Neural Networks: Architectures, Algorithms, and Applications*. Prentice Hall.

Gabrys, J. (2016). *Program Earth: Environmental Sensing Technology and the Making of a Computational Planet*. University of Minnesota Press.

Garcìa, J. A., Luengo, J., & Herrera, F. (2015). *Data preprocessing in data mining*. Springer.

Gitelman, L., & Jackson, V. (2013). Introduction. In L. Gitelman (Ed.), *Raw data is an Oxymoron* (pp. 1–14). MIT Press.

Ghosh, B., & Arora, S. (2021). Smart as (un)democratic? The making of a smart city imaginary in Kolkata, India. *Environment and Planning c: Politics and Space, 40*(1), 318–339. https://doi.org/10.1177/23996544211027583

Graham, S. (2005). Software-sorted geographies. *Progress in Human Geography, 29*(5), 562–580.

Howlett, D. (2013). ERP: SAP's journey in Cape Town. [Video Interview]. *Diginomica*. Retrieved from https://diginomica.com/erp-sap-journey-cape-town

Hughes, R. A., Heron, J., Sterne, J. A., & Tilling, K. (2019). Accounting for missing data in statistical analyses: Multiple imputation is not always the answer. *International Journal of Epidemiology, 48*(4), 1294–1304.

Interview 6. (November 2016). PDW, former city manager, Cape Town [in person].

Interview 13. (March 2018). DB, City manager, New Town [Online].

Interview 17. (March 2023). Smart City Consultant A. [Online].

Interview 19. (March 2023). Smart City Consultant B. [online].

King, A. (2016, October 20). Is Big Brother on the dark side of the smart city? *Irish Times.* https://www.irishtimes.com/news/science/is-big-brother-on-the-dark-side-of-the-smart-city-1.2836981

Kitchin, R. (2014). The real-time city? Big Data and Smart Urbanism. *GeoJournal, 79*(1), 1–14.

Kitchin, R. (2017) The realtimeness of smart cities. *Tecnoscienza, 8*(2),19-42

Lansdall-Welfare, T., Lampos, V., & Cristianini, N. (2012). Now-casting the mood of the nation. *Significance, 9*(4), 26–28.

Larose, D. T., & Larose, C. D. (2015). *Data mining and predictive analytics* (2nd ed.). Wiley.

Latour, B. (2005). *Reassembling the social: An introduction to Actor-Network Theory.* Oxford: Oxford University Press

Leszczyński, A. (2016). Speculative futures: Cities, data, and governance beyond smart urbanism. *Environment and Planning d: Society and Space, 34*(6), 1691–1710.

Lyon, D. (2018). *The culture of surveillance: Watching as a way of life.* Polity Press.

Mackenzie, A. (1997). The mortality of the virtual: Real-time, archive and dead-time in information networks. *Convergence, 3*(2), 59–71.

Marres, N., & Stark, D. (2020). Put to the test: For a new sociology of testing. *The British Journal of Sociology, 71*(3), 423–443. https://doi.org/10.1111/1468-4446.12746

Marvin, S., Luque-Ayala, A., & McFarlane, C. (2015). *Smart urbanism: Utopian vision or false dawn?* Routledge.

Mattern, S. (2013). Methodolatry and the art of measure. *Places Journal.* https://doi.org/10.22269/131031

McMullan, T. (2015, 23 July). What does the panopticon mean in the age of digital surveillance? *The Guardian.* https://www.theguardian.com/technology/2015/jul/23/panopticon-digital-surveillance-jeremy-bentham

McNeill, D. (2015). Global firms and smart technologies: IBM and the reduction of cities. *Transactions of the Institute of British Geographers, 40*(4), 562–574.

Morozov, E. (2013). *To save everything, click here: The folly of technological solutionism.* PublicAffairs.

114   I. ANTENUCCI

Murakami Wood, D. (2013). What is global surveillance? Towards a relational political economy of the global surveillant assemblage. *Geoforum, 49*, 317–326.

Murakami Wood, D., & McKinnon, R. (2019). Algorithmic regulation and the global city. *Urban Studies, 56*(13), 2729–2746.

O'Neill, C. (2016). *Weapons of math destruction: How big data increases inequality and threatens democracy.* Crown.

Pasquale, F. (2015). *The black box society: The secret algorithms that control money and information.* Harvard University Press.

Pasquinelli, M. (2017). Machines that morph logic: Neural networks and the distortion of the law. In M. Hildebrandt & K. de Vries (Eds.), *Privacy, Due Process and the Computational Turn* (pp. 3–25). Routledge.

Perrotta, C., & Williamson, B. (2018). The datafication of education: A critical approach to emerging data practices and infrastructures in digital education. *Learning, Media and Technology, 43*(1), 3–16.

Phadke, S., Khan, S., & Ranade, S. (2011). *Why loiter? Women and risk on Mumbai streets.* Penguin Books.

Raley, R. (2013). Dataveillance and countervailance. In L. Gitelman (Ed.) *Raw Data is an Oxymoron* (pp. 121–146). MIT Press

Rieder, B. (2017). Scrutinizing algorithms. In R. Hofmann & M. Riedl (Eds.), *Critical data studies* (pp. 67–81). Palgrave Macmillan.

Rosenberg, D. (2013). Data before the fact. In L. Gitelman (Ed.), *Raw data is an oxymoron.* MIT Press.

Rossiter, N. (2016). *Software, infrastructure, labor: A media theory of logistical nightmares.* Routledge.

Rouvroy, A., & Stiegler, B. (2016). The digital regime of truth: From the algorithmic governmentality to a new rule of law. *La Deleuziana: Online Journal of Philosophy, 3*, 6–29.

Samara, T. (2011). *Cape Town after apartheid: Crime and governance in the divided city.* University of Minnesota Press.

SAP News. (2017). *City of Cape Town customer video (programme EPIC).* Available at: https://www.youtube.com/watch?v=umW6z3C29RE&t=27s. (Accessed: 20 March 2020).

SAP. (2018). *SAP HANA Predictive Analysis Library (PAL).* https://help. sap.com/doc/86fb8d26952748debc8d08db756e6c1f/2.0.03/en-US/SAP_ HANA_Predictive_Analysis_Library_PAL_en.pdf

Seaver, N. (2014). Knowing algorithms [Conference paper]. *Media in Transition 8*, Cambridge, MA. http://nickseaver.net/papers/seaverMiT8.pdf

Smart City Proposal Annexures, n.d., http://164.100.161.224/upload/upload files/files/Annexures_Kolkata.pdf

Smith, J. P., & Mortimer, A. (2017). The citizen-centric city. Improving safety and security [Power point presentation]. Available at: http://www.afsug. com/library/documents/saphila_2017_presentations/STREAM%202_P03_ Alderman%20JP%20Smith%20Andrew%20Mortimer.pdf (Accessed: 10 June 2020).

Steyerl, H. (2018). A sea of data: Pattern recognition and corporate animism (Forked Version). In C. Apprich, W. Chun, F. Cramer, H. Steyerl (Eds.) *Pattern Discrimination* (pp. 1–22). Meson Press.

Tufekci, Z. (2014). Engineering the public: Big data, surveillance and computational politics. *First Monday*, 19(7). https://doi.org/10.5210/fm.v19i7. 4901

Van Dijck, J. (2014). Datafication, dataism and dataveillance: Big Data between scientific paradigm and ideology. *Surveillance & society*, 12(2), 197–208.

Weisberg, M. (2013). *Simulation and similarity: Using models to understand the world*. Oxford University Press.

Weltevrede, E., Helmond, A., & Gerlitz, C. (2014). The politics of real-time: A device perspective on social media platforms and search engines. *Theory, Culture & Society*, 31(6), 125–150.

CHAPTER 5

From Land to Data: Money in the Smart City

Inside Candor Techspace, a young crowd flows between the white buildings, flower beds, and fountains. They wear badges and stroll around looking at their smartphones. The complex offers plenty of open sitting areas, shops, and restaurants, but many head outside the gates, towards the informal food stalls that are lined up along the road. Just over the fence, a couple of cows graze peacefully on the well-maintained lawn. A 45,40-acre campus in New Town Kolkata, Candor is home to multinational tech firms like Accenture, Capgemini, Tata Consultancy Services, and Cognisant. One of the first IT Special Economic Zones established in Rajarhat, it sits on land that once belonged to the farmers of the nearby village of Chack Pachuria and was forcibly acquired by the government in the early 2000s. Many of the dispossessed landowners now support themselves by running food shops around the Candor gates, always under the threat of imminent displacement (Dey et al., 2013). Developed by Indian firm Unitech, the campus opened for business in 2005 under the name of Infospace. Global investment firm Brookfield acquired Candor in 2014, along with other IT developments in Gurugram and Noida, reportedly in a USD900 million deal (Srivastava, 2018). A major finance player with a portfolio of more than USD285 billion assets, Brookfield's investments count over USD5 billion in infrastructures, office parks, and private equity. The timing of the Candor acquisition was ideal, just before the Modi administration launched the Smart City Mission. The story of

© The Author(s), under exclusive license to Springer Nature
Switzerland AG 2025
I. Antenucci, *Future-proofed*,
https://doi.org/10.1007/978-3-031-86429-2_5

the Candor SEZ says a lot of New Town Kolkata. It lays out a path that begins with land grabbing, new enclosures, and the dispossession of local communities, and leads to the speculations of global finance capital on the smart city to come.

So far, this book has explored different angles of speculative urbanism in the smart cities of New Town Kolkata and Cape Town, from narratives, to testing practices, to algorithmic security. This chapter charts how financial speculation and extractivism, in their different forms, contribute to shaping the smart city. It begins by mapping the relationships between data, value, extraction, and speculation that have emerged in recent critical literature. Moving across different examples from Cape Town and Kolkata, I then discuss the instruments and processes—Special Economic Zones and gentrification, financial ventures and startups, platform labour management and market modelling—through which urban digitalisation is monetised and speculated upon.

DATA, VALUE, EXTRACTIONS (S)

Write smart cities, read data mining. And data, as we read everywhere, 'is the new oil': a critical source of value in the age of what has been termed digital, algorithmic, platform, or surveillance capitalism. Despite their differences, all these definitions place data extractivism at the core of industrial processes and value generation. As Evgeny Morozov puts it, in the industry of digital technology users are the 'valuable stocks of data' that companies seek to drain: 'either to fuel their advertising-heavy business models—more and better data yields higher advertising earnings per user—or they need it in order to develop advanced modes of artificial intelligence centred around the principle of "deep learning"; here, the diversity of data inputs—and the ability to leverage millions of users to teach different behaviours to the machine—comes in handy' (2017, p. 2). Over the past decade, platforms such as Uber, Airbnb, Deliveroo, and many more, have emerged as major actors of data extraction. Platforms dominate a new market of services—from booking a restaurant to finding a date—as well as of digitally mediated precarious labour—car drivers, delivery riders, chores on demand, etc. Especially in their early days, these companies have been packaged with benign definitions, such as the 'sharing' or 'gig' economy, suggesting a gentle and humane business model based on workers' independence and fair technological mediation between users. But as Nick Srnicek (2016) makes clear, platforms are not alternative to capitalism. They are instead peculiar capitalist players, which draw their growing power from computing technologies. More and more, it has come to light how platforms leverage their algorithmic infrastructures to exploit the vulnerability of workers and coerce them into acting as independent contractors, with no rights or protection. At the same time, users who engage with their services are tapped in as data pools to feed targeted advertising and as free labour to train new machine learning applications. Cities with a high concentration of digital infrastructures and tech-savvy dwellers offer the best conditions for platforms to invest and test their technologies. For Jathan Sadowski (2019) there are six paths through which data generates value. These include profiling and targeting people, optimising operations and systems, managing things, modelling probabilities, building stuff, and growing the value of assets. As we will shortly see in this chapter, all of these forms of value extraction somehow play out in smart cities, linking the monetisation of data to the broader forms of extraction from the urban environment. Modelling, however, is particularly crucial. Indeed, with Sadowski (2019), it is important to stress that not all the value extracted from data is necessarily monetary or, at least, not immediately. In fact, as this chapter will argue, the valorisation of data in smart cities is inscribed in relations that are inherently speculative. This means that what is not immediately turned into money is involved in the creation of future money. Modelling—which in the world of commercial platforms takes the form of customer profiling, targeted advertising, customised discounts or payment plans, and more—is the specific technique through which data are used to anticipate the future and generate value. The use of data mining for value extraction goes back a long way. Louise Amoore (2013) narrates how the first systems of data mining were developed in the early nineties for marketing purposes, when IBM researcher Rakesh Agrawal provided British retailer Marks & Spencer with algorithms that were capable of unearthing patterns among large volumes of commercial transactions (pp. 39–43).

Today, Agrawal's algorithms are the lifeblood of business processes. In the previous chapter we saw many of the flaws and controversial implications of the modelling practices used in the domain of security and governance. Similarly, modelling pervasively employed across a broad spectrum of commercial practices—from marketing to logistical 'optimisation' to workforce management—can have troubling effects, from privacy violations to the point of behavioural manipulation (Degli Esposti, 2014). A rich body of scholarship has drawn attention to the ways in which the algorithmic management of workers has further enhanced exploitation, and we will see more of this later in this chapter. At the same time, customer profiling might be no less disturbing, working as a predatory strategy that deliberately targets vulnerable subjects. For example, as Cathy O'Neill (2016) documents, for-profit colleges and loan companies in the US target specific profiles such as the poorest zip codes, low education, low-wage jobs, single mothers, and recent trauma, with misleading ads on Facebook and Google. Prospective students are lured into taking out government loans to buy overpriced courses that are worth nothing on the job market. Jobless parents are offered short-term loans with impossible interest rates. This perpetuates a cycle of indebtedness and marginalisation that is algorithmically engineered with great precision. Not all modelling techniques are put to work to such predatory and devastating results. Yet, what matters for the sake of this analysis, is that modelling—anticipating and possibly shaping user's behaviour—is a core component of the business processes of platforms.

The drainage of personal data and their algorithmic engineering is a form of what Andrea Fumagalli (2011; 2015) defines as the full subsumption of life in biocognitive capitalism. Since the 1970s, critical Marxist scholars have flagged a tendency, in the post-Fordist transformation of production and labour, to erase the boundaries between productive and reproductive time/space and to exploit the whole range of human resources, and even of life itself, from biological information to emotions and fun (Lazzarato, 1997; Morini & Fumagalli, 2010). The behavioural manipulation performed by algorithms becomes, in this perspective, a tool of social subjugation whereby personal information, hopes, desires, and vulnerabilities are captured and then exploited to the fullest extent.

If data extractivism is crucial to smart cities, it is not disconnected from other extractive processes. Authors like Sandro Mezzadra and Brett Neilson (2017), and Kate Crawford and Vladan Joler (2018), have shown that data extractivism is not entirely an invention of the digital industry. It rather needs to be associated with the long history of extractive practices that runs through colonialism and the globalisation of capitalism over at least the last four centuries. Nick Couldry and Ulises A. Mejias (2018) see a continuum between the systematic dispossession of land, resources, and bodies, of historical colonialism (and, more broadly, capitalism and modernity), and the excavation of life that platforms perform today. This perspective invites us to consider how data extractivism remains intimately linked to, and dependent on them, earthly extractive practices, including mining and drilling for rare minerals, oil, and gas, which the digital industry consumes voraciously.

Smart cities are made up of sensors, servers, and computers, which are made up of plastic and minerals. The damage caused by mining, drilling, and fracking is massive and ranges from the erosion of the earth's crust to the poisoning of water, air, soil, and humans, to the CO_2 emissions caused by the container shipping companies that move resources from suppliers to buyers (Crawford & Joler, 2018, drawing on Schlanger, 2018). Sensors, chips, and batteries contain toxic minerals such as mercury, cadmium, beryllium, lithium, and lead; minerals, like copper and gold, which can be recycled; and, of course, plastic. Vincent Mosco notes (2015, p. 113, drawing on Acaroglu, 2013) that a large part of the e-waste produced in the Global North is dumped in the poorer areas of Africa, China, Southeast Asia, Eastern Europe, and Latin America. Here, an informal recycling industry has workers (often children) scraping garbage in highly unsafe conditions, searching for components that they can sell for a few dollars.

This excursus has made clear how smart city projects might be sold as equitable and sustainable, but are in fact inextricable from planetary processes of exploitation and environmental degradation. At the same time, the intense forms of data extractivism that concentrate in smart cities are only possible within a broader, sedimented framework of material extractive practices. As Couldry and Meijas (2018) argue, life and social relationships need to be reconfigured in ways that are amenable to extraction. Zooming back on the urban scale, this is the case for cities as well: urban environments need to be prepared and rearranged in modalities that enable data extraction. This is the work of smart city projects that are, on their part, grafted upon stories of extraction and speculation over land and the built environment that predate and prefigure the smart city.

Land Grabbing, Gentrification, and the Work of Finance

Special Economic Zones for the IT industry were established in Rajarhat about ten years before the smart city, but turned out to be instrumental for the project. The New Town Smart City Proposal strongly leveraged the presence of tech hubs as an indicator of the city's economic potential and technological advancement. Companies have been consulted as stakeholders in the planning of infrastructures and policies. Candor Techspace tenants Accenture and Tata Consultancy Services, as well as other firms quartered in New Town such as Wipro, Intel, SAP, Oracle, and IBM, have contracts for the implementation of specific components of the Pan City solution. As Chapter 1 documents, the smart city may still be more narrative than reality, but its appeal to investors was almost instantaneous. One of my interlocutors, RC, a senior executive in a major Indian property development company, made some interesting observations about this point. The company has a broad portfolio, spanning across West Bengal and India, and had already invested considerably in the creation of New Town, well before the smart city plans had been made public. When I first spoke to RC, in 2015, the smart city was still very much an abstract idea. He welcomed me into his office, inside one of New Town's semi-fortified business enclaves, where several layers of security filter the contacts between the corporate world and the city outside. At that time, RC's main professional concern was, understandably, how to attract new investors to complete the construction of New Town and how to drag it out of the purgatory in which it was stuck. The company RC works for had managed to complete three properties in the area—one business park and two residential developments—of which only one, the one we were sitting in, had a reasonable number of tenants. He expressed cautious optimism about the idea of building a smart city. He wouldn't buy the hype, and didn't believe it was likely that 'they will build a new Singapore here in four or five years' (Personal conversation 4, 2015). However, in his view the smart city project could at least give the place 'a vision, an identity' that he felt were missing, and that it would help New Town fit into global trends of investment. In RC's words, 'This place has failed so far because it was never top-tier. It wanted to be top-tier, but it was always second, third-tier'. This related to what he saw as the poor choices made by planners and politicians, who never adequately analysed the real market opportunities in the area; or who deliberately pursued what they knew was an enterprise bound to fail, because they were corrupt. Against this background, and in RC's view, the smart city was possibly the last chance for companies that had invested in the area to reposition themselves within fresh and more appealing marketing strategies.

As a matter of fact, the inclusion of New Town Kolkata in the Smart City Mission programme in 2015 quickly fired up investors. Remaining plots of lands began to sell quickly. In 2017, there were over 4,000 applicants for the 100 residential plots put up for sale by HIDCO ('HIDCO starts lottery', 2017). Luxury brands made offers for space to open flagship stores in a dedicated retail hub, a seven-acre plot in Action Area II. And in August 2018, Banerjee's government laid the foundational stone for the Bengal Silicon Valley Hub. When I heard from RC again in 2022, seven years after New Town was officially included in the Smart City Mission, he was still sceptical about the project's real chances. Yet he acknowledged a tangible enthusiasm about New Town among financial circuits. 'All the talk' about the smart city to come and the government's commitment to large investments had brought back both firms and private investors. After long years of crisis, the real estate market was going up again. RC kept his doubts that the Bengal Silicon Valley's would ever become a major tech hub for Asia, but he concedes that it is proving a real estate booster (Personal conversation 5, October 2022).

As seen in Chapter 1, smart city narratives and projects are strongly performative. Regardless of the actual progresses of constructions, they carry out economic practices, prompting investments and financial operations that bet on the urban future. Well before the smart city or the Bengal Silicon Valley turn into reality—if they ever do—they are already generating value along a chain of land appropriation, financial instruments, ventures, and rent. In different forms, something similar happened in Cape Town. Here, rather than greenfield developments, it is the project of clustering startups into the existing metropolitan area that has driven urban transformations, with a substantial involvement of venture capital and equity funds, both homegrown and global. Over the past ten years, South African investment firms have increasingly targeted the tech sector. A survey conducted by the South African Venture Capital Association (SAVCA, 2017) showed that the value of venture capital investments, made during 2016 was R872 million (approximately USD61 million), 134% more than in 2015, when it amounted to R372 million (USD26 million). Forty-one per cent of investments were in the Cape Town region, and 30% of the whole was directed to the ICT sector (SAVCA, 2017). To give just a few examples, Knife Capital, a Cape Town- based growth equity firm, has supported local AI-focused companies such as Data Prophet, Quicket, and OrderTalk, in scaling up their business from

124 I. ANTENUCCI

South Africa to larger markets in UK and US.[1] 4Di Capital is behind the growth of Lukmani, a fire detection system for informal communities; LifeQ, which provides insurance and wearable devices companies with a platform for health monitoring and personalised risk analytics; Sensor Networks, a home IoT platform business with a focus on the insurance industry; and the list goes on. Far from virtual, these financial operations have a socio-spatial impact on the urban fabric. In Chapter 1, I introduced Woodstock, a formerly industrial neighbourhood west of the Cape Town CBD, which has been turned into a startup hub. Since 2010, the price of properties there has increased by 100%. One by one, the old mills and abandoned warehouses have been purchased by property developers and equity shareholders, and now host co-working spaces, corporate offices, gourmet restaurants, and designer boutiques. The legacy of this working class, ethnically mixed community, which resisted apartheid segregation, is still partially visible in the handful of second-hand shops, workshops (real ones), and not yet redeveloped housing blocks. Yet a large portion of the residents has been kicked out by aggressive real estate politics and the influx of upper middle-class residents with scarce tolerance for the aesthetics and habits of their lower-income neighbours. Exemplar in this sense is the story of Bromwell Street's residents: ten families who have been fighting against eviction in court since 2016, after property developers Woodstock Hub bought the cottages they had been renting for decades. As tech companies, affluent crowds and extensive surveillance have moved in, Woodstock has become one of the symbols of gentrification in Cape Town. Finance capital is running the show here, pumping money into young companies and real estate speculation alike.

Kolkata, by contrast, is not a startup capital. In India, the title sits firmly in the hands of Bangalore, followed by Hyderabad, Noida, and Gurugram. And despite the rhetoric of smartness, New Town has so far occupied a subordinate position in the geography of the tech industry. Rather than research hubs and headquarters, the township typically accommodates company branches devoted to ordinary and repetitive tasks such as business process outsourcing or beta testing (Dey, 2013; Rossiter, 2016). New Town tech campuses seem to be concerned, more than with innovation, with tapping into the young, cheap workforce from nearby

---

[1] Data Prophet is a startup specialised in machine learning systems for business; Quicket produces cloud-based ticketing solution; and OrderTalk is a software for online ordering for restaurants.

colleges such as St. Xavier and Techno India. Graduates in information technology, computer science, and software engineering programmes are increasingly competing for internships and jobs at companies such as Wipro, Accenture, Infosys, TCS, etc., only to find themselves stuck in positions they are overqualified for, and carrying out repetitive tasks in highly pressured working conditions, with low prospects of further learning or career advancement. If not a nest for tech startups, New Town seems to be at least a good market for them, especially in the sectors of transport, mostly with Uber, and food delivery, with Zomato, Swiggy, Uber Eats, Foodpanda, and others. Especially the young tech workforce of New Town rely increasingly on these platforms. Zomato, in particular, targeted New Town, as one of the broader metropolitan areas of Kolkata, in 2011, for the first stage of its expansion, which included five other major Indian cities: Delhi, Pune, Chennai, Mumbai, and Bangalore. Between 2010 and 2013, the platform raised approximately USD16.7 million from Info Edge India, giving them a 57.9% stake in Zomato. From 2013 to 2018, the company raised about another USD500 million from various investors, including Sequoia Capital, Info Edge India, Vy Capital, Temasek, and Alibaba's affiliate, Ant Financial, which owns now 10% of the company. Since 2012, Zomato has expanded into 24 countries outside India and acquired 12 startups around the world, mostly in the food-tech sector, including American food portal, Urbanspoon. In 2018, Zomato acquired TechEagle Innovations, a company that works on drones, with the aim of introducing drone-based food delivery in India ('Zomato buys Tech Eagle', 2018). In 2021, the company shut down most of its global branches to focus exclusively on India and the United Arab Emirates. Such injections of financial capital do not come without strings attached: investors dictate strategies that look apt to maximise their future exits. Often, startups are pushed towards a speedy growth, which might inflate short-term returns for investors in the form of exit or shares value, but compromises sustainability, innovation, and profitability in the long term (Kenney & Zysman, 2019; Lazonick, 2014). Uber is a notorious example in this respect, having expanded and run at loss for years. Thanks to a continuous inflow of capital, the 'unicorn' was able to pursue a strategy of market domination, culminating in an Initial Public Offer (IPO) that was expected to be largest in history (only to glaringly fail predictions in the end). But to keep together relentless expansion and lack of profitability, some costs must be cut to reduce losses (Srnicek, 2016). Who pays the price of these crusades for market hegemony? Largely, the answer seems to be: the workers. Later in this chapter we will see how cropping workers' wages and squeezing as much value as possible out of them through algorithmic forms of discipline and control is at the core of platform operations. Destitute workers, broken entrepreneurs, and a disrupted economic system are what this vicious intimacy between startups and financialisation often leaves behind.

The urban environment is not spared either. In the wake of the 2008 global crisis and later, it has become more and more appreciable that financialisation carries disciplinary, performative, and often destructive effects across a broad societal spectrum (Marazzi, Lebedeva, & Gimsey, 2011; Lazzarato, 2015; Fields, 2017). With ramifications into every aspect of life, finance capital has the power to condition not only the industrial operations but the very fabric of neighbourhoods, cities, habits, and even emotions, through the binomials of debt and speculation. We all have in mind the abandoned suburbs and the rows of houses for sale in the aftermath of the US subprime crisis. But beyond that, a wide range of financial instruments and networks are increasingly affecting the production of the urban space (see, among others, Fainstein, 2016; Rouanet & Halbert, 2016; Weber, 2010)—i.e. 'the design, construction, exploitation and ownership of the urban built environment' (Halbert & Attuyer, 2016, p. 1)—triggering, and feeding on, enclosing and expulsion processes. In New Town, the incomplete construction sites, empty buildings, abandoned land plots, and slums are sobering manifestations of the impact of financialisation. The real estate initiatives and the Special Economic Zones of the early 2000s have never fulfilled their promise of creating a leading IT hub, an exclusive residential suburb or 'a new Singapore'. Instead, the township has moved on from speculation to speculation—the smart city and the Bengal Silicon Valley are the latest ones—in an attempt to amend previous failures. New investors buy the debts of older investors, while banks and equity funds step in every time, to fuel the chain of loans, rate interests, and derivatives. On the other side of this chain remain the destructions of the livelihoods of thousands of local households and masses of dispossessed people who struggle to make a living in the informal sector.

The painful, startup-driven transformation of Woodstock and the IT enclaves and half-empty gated communities of New Town might be geographically, aesthetically, and socially very distant, but have more in common than meets the eye. In both cases, smart city plans and narratives have fuelled, and have been fuelled by, financial speculations. Dispossession, expulsion, and aggressive rent extraction from the urban fabric emerge here, albeit along different paths—'old school' land grabbing in Kolkata, gentrification in Cape Town—which are similarly triggered by a conjuncture of financial operations and socio-technical imaginaries of smart cities.

Platforms and Their Discontents

On the morning of June 26, 2018, a long convoy of shiny sedans was parked in the middle of busy Somerset Road in Green Point, Cape Town, blocking the traffic in a strategic area of the city centre. Drivers from Uber and its main rival in South Africa, Taxify, were protesting against exploitation from their 'bosses'—the platforms—and asking for labour regulations and protection in their sector. The police fired stun grenades to break up the blockade and two drivers were arrested. Later that year, in November, the app drivers went on strike again, for several days. This time they released a statement which compared their conditions to slavery, accusing government officers of corruption. They announced the end of negotiations with Uber and Taxify because 'slavery is a system that only deserves abolishment without compromise' (Mebelengwa, 2018).

Only a few days earlier, their Uber and Ola colleagues in Kolkata had put their apps offline and blocked the streets, raising similar claims. Faced with a surge in fuel prices, e-hailing companies had cut off minimum fares for passengers, while increasing the fees that drivers had to pay to them. Additionally, some drivers had their accounts unilaterally blocked by Uber. Company officials explained this was because the drivers had received negative feedback, as well as because the 'in-built processes' of the platform identified the profiles of drivers as 'not suited to provide the best service' (Chakraborty & Ghosh, 2018).

Uber is a pioneer of e-hailing services and an icon of the platform economy. It has opened the field for a number of competitors around the world—Lyft, Waze, the above-mentioned Ola and Taxify, Bolt, and more. Through its software and hardware apparatus, it orchestrates and controls more than 18 million rides per day across all continents. The extraction of data is critical to Uber as to all other platforms. Data are used to manage workers, improve algorithms, and offer new services and products. They can also be sold to other companies. For Srnicek (2016), Uber is a relevant example of a 'lean' platform: a business that minimises the fixed costs of workforce and infrastructures and maximises the outsourcing of labour and fixed capital, while retaining control over the software that enables transactions between workers and customers. It also controls the multiple types of data extracted concerning traffic, clients' habits, route patterns, car performances, and more. Yet along with the relevance of technologies, as Srnicek argues, the critical resource that lean platforms really rely on for their revenue strategies is surplus labour. Large pools of unemployed or precarious workers, both presented and formally registered as independent contractors, are in fact forced into self-employment. They work for low wages and without any protection or benefits, as exposed by the Uber drivers in Kolkata and Cape Town.

Uber started its operations in Cape Town in 2013, and in Kolkata in 2014. In both cities, success was fast and tangible. Quickly, in both cities the service became more and more a staple of urban life and was incorporated into local smart city narratives. In Cape Town, Uber rides are definitely part of the daily routines of middle-class residents of the central areas of the city. Cheap and reliable, Uber is widely used to travel to work, go out at night, reach beaches, and even to do the school drop-off. The townships, however, as areas of poverty, low access to technology, and high crime rates, are typically not on the platform's map. In Kolkata, Uber has grown increasingly popular, especially among young professionals, but competition with traditional taxis and *autos* remains strong. The platform procedures, designed in and for North American cities, turned out to be too rigid for the context. For example, the frequent absence of street names and civic numbers in the city required some form of beyond-the-platform communication between drivers and riders. This was a barrier to non-Bengali speakers, including myself, because most drivers did not speak English; but also a nuisance for local customers, who were often forced to long negotiations over the phone before they could get their ride. Besides, the obligation to pay online, via credit card, was so at odds with the local habit of bargaining for taxi rides, that eventually the company allowed Indian drivers to accept cash. At any rate, Uber quickly became a convenient way to reach and move around New Town Kolkata, which is poorly served by public transport, and often seen as too remote by taxi drivers. Particularly the young IT workers made use of the platform regularly. In both Kolkata and Cape Town, Uber regularly came up during almost every interview or informal conversation. It was mentioned as tangible evidence that the city was getting better at technology and 'smarter' overall. Although my interlocutors would not generally agree on what makes a city smart, they would all agree Uber was one of those things. The fact that a mere click would materialise a car and a driver within minutes seemed to synthesise many different elements of the smart city narrative, including the extensive distribution of technologies throughout the population, job opportunities and economic development, efficient transport, and, last but not least, a certain aesthetic.

The reference to slavery made by the Capetonians Uber drivers is strikingly at odds with the types of discourses that Uber has mobilised in his marketing campaigns around the world, and that drivers and customers seemed to absorb, at least in the early stage. As Andrea Pollio illustrates in his research into Uber drivers in Cape Town (2019), the e-hailing company packaged its entry into the South African market with narratives of empowerment and emancipation through entrepreneurship, fitting into a broader public discourse intersecting development and neoliberalism, as seen in Chap. 1. Drivers were highly motivated by the aspects of self-management and independence, despite facing hardships such as debts, long shifts, and low incomes. Uber worked its way through Cape Town by incorporating and leveraging tropes that were rooted in the post-apartheid developmental politics and social imaginary. The company successfully marketed itself as a key player for the promotion of the city's world-class status and attractiveness in the touristic market. At the same time, Uber aligned itself with specific 'ethics of care' (Pollio, 2019, p. 766) by partnering with NGOs and supporting firefighters and residents affected by the fires of the summer of 2015. In addition, Uber drew upon the increasingly influential idea in the country's political debate that structural poverty and segregation could be overcome through (self, in this case) entrepreneurship (Pollio, 2019). Not too dissimilarly, when it started business in Kolkata, in 2014, Uber recruited a pool of driving partners by aggressively campaigning on a narrative of individual empowerment and upward mobility. The idea of an entrepreneurial way out of poverty was not new, as microfinance institutions had been in business since the early 2000s, but had coexisted with the long-standing strategies of poverty relief, ministered through networks of patronage linked to political parties and by a large NGO industry. However, after the BJP party came to power in 2014, with a strongly pro-market agenda, discourses and programmes to promote individual entrepreneurship—such as the 'Start up India' funding scheme—gained more momentum.

Uber's marketing strategies focused on the promise of an attractive, reliable source of income, which could lift drivers out of poverty and enable them to pursue their own ambitions, such as starting a family or paying for higher education. Potential drivers were also offered a social upgrade to the middle-class and the status of entrepreneur, symbolised by self-management and the ownership of a car. The stories of successful drivers featured on the company's blog (Uber, 2016) depict joining the platform as a game-changer that would allow individuals to unlock their self-entrepreneurial potential and begin to climb up the socio-economic ladder, through their unique skills and hard work. In short, in both Cape Town and Kolkata, Uber marketed itself by adjusting its storyline to site-specific tropes and values. At the same time, though, Uber had to somehow create its own labour supply. When it started its operations in the US and in European cities, Uber could count on the fact that most people—even low-income or unemployed—commonly have a car available, and might be willing to use it to make extra money, or to make a living out of it in absence of better options. In Kolkata and Cape Town, by contrast, low-income people hardly own cars as idly assets. In other words, to launch its services in those cities Uber had to put potential drivers in a condition to drive in the first place. To provide drivers with cars, the platform had to integrate existing circuits of informal economies into financial protocols. For example, the drivers that I met in India came from lowly skilled, low-wage, and unregulated jobs, such as cooking in street food stalls and driving trucks. As part of its efforts to 'bring entrepreneurship to the Indian grassroots' (Uber, 2014) and to introduce individual entrepreneurs into the formal workforce and banking system (Uber, 2016), Uber partnered with several Indian lending companies, as well as with Tata Motors, to launch a financing scheme that would enable drivers to buy their own cars. Hoping for a quick improvement of their working and living conditions, many drivers took out loans, but they did that mostly through informal networks—kinship or local middlemen—rather than through the Uber-sponsored financial schemes. In Cape Town, as the platform recruits drivers, it also incorporates networks of kinship or patronage through which 'cars are sourced, officials are bribed to release driving permits, neighbourhoods are "assigned," circuits of protection are brokered and other jobs are made sustainable' (Pollio, 2019, p. 7). Pollio also draws attention to the multiple transactions that drivers activate across, around, and against the platform in the attempt to maximise their revenues and somehow to reverse their asymmetric power relationship with the algorithm.

At some point, however, the contrast between Uber's marketing campaigns and the real working conditions of the drivers became explosive. A report from 2016 describes Cape Town drivers working 24-hour shifts and sleeping in their cars in a parking lot near the airport while waiting for long trips, yet still struggling to make a living (De Greef, 2016). Similar conditions are lamented by Indian drivers, many of whom are trapped by loans they can't repay (Dhillon, 2018). It is no surprise, then, that drivers have collectively come to identify Uber as an exploitative force and the self-employment narrative as a trap. In both the Kolkata and Cape Town protests, drivers were clearly trying to humanise their counterpart in many ways: by addressing their company supervisors—unresponsive—or by marching to the company offices—closed. And unsurprisingly so, since drivers were fighting against decisions and procedures that are far beyond labour negotiations in the traditional sense. Obscure and unaccountable, Uber's algorithms perform functions of tracking, ranking, profiling, and anticipation that are not dissimilar from those of the security platforms examined in the previous chapter. In the past few years, Uber workers have repeatedly attempted to make some sense of the formulas and strings of code responsible for their poor working conditions. According to official Uber sources, which are generous in detailing their technological developments, the machine learning apparatus that connects riders and drivers calculates several factors, including driver rating, customer rating, destination, expected surge pricing, and traffic, in its attempts to optimise the service for both parties. Not everyone agrees with such explanation. In 2017, a post on the forum uberpeople.net—an independent community for drivers—from a San Francisco member proposed a different explanation of how Uber matches drivers and riders. In their view, the company has tweaked the algorithms over time, to maximise its gains at the expense of drivers:

'UBER will assign the trips in a way that they can pay less. Experienced drivers will always be more expensive, and new drivers are cheaper to UBER, because over time, one learns to maximise earnings, however, this will also run against the experienced drivers eventually, as they get assigned less profitable trips or less trips overall. (…) Basically, getting UBER rides is no longer a "fair and random" affair, where once upon a time the closest driver is paired to a request, instead, they dispatch them in a way that they will pay less while fulfilling the rides. It's hard to beat the algorithm – the longer hours for less money is not an accident, not a full result of over-hiring drivers, but a careful adjustment on trips being assigned' (Silent_Philosodriver, 2017).

There is no evidence, of course, that this hypothesis of a malign algorithm is correct, and Uber firmly denies it. What is evident, however, is the increasing frustration and perceived unfairness that Uber drivers across the globe are experiencing from their algorithmic boss. The Uber workers' protest leads back to finance's role in the booming of tech companies. At the time of the protests, Uber was preparing for its IPO, set for May 2019, which experts expected to be the largest in history (and which eventually ended up in a remarkable loss for the company). Despite its global expansion and tremendous estimated value, at the time of the IPO the company was famous for never having generated revenues. Corporate management had presented this as a specific market strategy, aimed at securing a hegemonic position in the market. Yet investors, which include several funds, such as Benchmark Capital, Softbank, Google Ventures, and Lowercase Capital, potentially had an interest to reduce the company's losses, in view of the imminent IPO. Consequently, investors pushed the company to adjust its business model and reduce costs. This would explain the abrupt cut in drivers' wages. In other words, the command of finance might be the force behind the (malign, for some) algorithms and the loss of revenues for drivers.

Platform capitalism is deeply intertwined with the making of smart cities in terms of narratives, infrastructures, and practices. Smart cities are—at least in the hopes of their planners—made of platforms, which anticipate and manage the future in advance. Modelling—from real-time to long-term scenarios—is as vital to Uber (and to other business platforms) as it is to emergency rooms and security platforms. The proliferation of digital infrastructures and startups corresponds to the multiplication of platform labour, such as Uber of course, but also food delivery, cleaners on demand, and other types of informal jobs that have gone digital, and whose income and working hours are algorithmically determined. The experiences of Uber's workers, also echoed in broader research (Munn, 2017), indicate that these algorithms operate as forces of labour control, which actively seek to monitor, profile, discipline, manipulate, discriminate, and punish workers. Uber operations are based on an incessant series of algorithmic speculations—of rides' demand, price surges, traffic, best routes, and drivers' behaviours—which aim to extract the maximum possible value from all the involved elements.

Michelangelo, Uber's machine learning platform, crunches petabytes of data from numerous different sources, including users' apps; GPS; cars; cameras; sensors; maps; business partners, such as Google, Facebook, and Spotify; weather forecasts; news; and financial institutions. These data are processed to generate models for car dispatching, dynamic pricing, anomaly detection, extreme event forecasting, and other business operations. Overall, Uber acts as a private, extensive platform of surveillance and preemption, not only for its drivers but also for customers and, more broadly, for the city. This suggests a convergence of techniques, tools, and logics in smart cities that cuts across security and economics. In other words, speculation—as a way of *prefiguring and producing* the future at once—is transversal to urban governance and value extraction. Public and private platforms are increasingly organised through similar architectures of speculative calculations and anticipatory action.

URBAN MINING

In their work on the smart city of Songdo, Halpern et al. (2013) argue that the project is driven by a logic that seeks to manipulate and monetise every bit of human attention: 'The developers, financiers and media boosters of this city argue for a speculative space ahead of its time that operates at the synaptic level of its inhabitants' (p. 279). The city is planned as a totalising sensory environment, where every movement is monitored, and every infrastructural component can double as an interface for the provision of services, i.e. domestic walls turn into screens for weather reports or telemedicine. Songdo is an experiment in new technologies and business models, concerning how to turn data into profit to the fullest extent; but, perhaps more importantly, to create solutions that can be exported and sold to other cities. It is, in short, 'a test bed for a form of urban life that is itself the product' (2013, p. 290): incessantly connected, monitored, and fed new services and commodities based on algorithmic predictions. Songdo, a smart city designed and built from scratch, is of course an extreme case. In most cases, smart city projects develop in piecemeal, layered, and fragmented ways; they build on, integrate, and (often) conflict with existing infrastructure. Yet one does not need a Songdo to come across technologies that seek to manipulate and monetise the attention, interactions, and emotions of urban residents. These are, in fact, standard platforms operations, increasingly part of the mundane digital transactions of our daily lives. We just saw how one of the major commercial platforms, Uber, is using its computing architecture to maximise the extraction of value from data, at the expense of drivers. But Uber is only one among an ever-expanding mosaic of applications that make up the fabric of smart cities. The rampant datafication of urban environments provides immense opportunities for those who are in a position to capture and process information.

Successful platforms turn their names into verbs. In Kolkata, over the past few years, it has become more and more common to *uber* somewhere and to *zomato* restaurants—at least for those who own a smartphone and can afford to eat out. I mentioned Indian food-tech company Zomato earlier in this chapter, as an example of the nexus of finance capital and tech startups. Zomato started in India in 2008, as a restaurant finder: a catalogue featuring details, menus, photos, reviews, and other information about restaurants in each area. Since then, the app has added many more services, including online booking, food delivery, and membership programmes. Over the following decade, Zomato expanded to 24 countries and more than 1000 cities around the world. In 2021, however, it ceased its operations in all countries except India and the United Arab Emirates. Similar to Uber, cities with a high concentration of technology and lively economies are the business backbone of Zomato. In major Indian cities, including Kolkata and New Town, Zomato is one of the go-to apps when it comes to choosing a restaurant and, more recently, to book and order food online. In 2017, Zomato introduced the Gold membership, which provides perks and discounts in selected restaurants to those who subscribe to the programme for six or twelve months.

As it provides information about restaurants and food delivery services, Zomato deploys a broad range of techniques of identification, monitoring, and profiling. When using the app, user's location is registered and tracked. Bespoke recommendation for restaurants are generated by combining the user's previous searches, ratings, and reviews, as well as further data from third parties. The list is organised into categories, such as 'Takeaway' or 'Drinks and Nightlife', which are regularly updated. Alternatively, users can browse a list of 'Collections', which suggests different themes such as 'Trending this Week', 'Hidden Gems', 'Romantic', 'Best Breakfast', 'Sunset', etc. Or they can make their own search, using filters such as distance, rating, type of cuisine, occasion, etc. Users can post reviews and photos of their meals; and follow, and be followed by, other 'foodies'. Zomato users must provide personal details in order to be identified. Their credentials are re-validated on any new access. When using the platform's services, all activities—searches, reviews, transactions, etc.—are monitored and tracked to feed further customised suggestions and offers. In an interview with an Indian online magazine, the leader of the Data Science and Analytics team at Zomato, Naresh Mehta, describes how the company has powerfully leveraged machine learning analytics to boost its business (Bathia, 2018). Metha explains that machine learning applications range from logistics optimisation—call centre and driver fleet capacity planning, delivery time prediction, and supply prioritisation—to user experience—User Generated Content moderation, aesthetic scoring of photos and image classification, Natural Language Processing of reviews to extract key information from text, payment fraud prediction, search and listing, and more. These applications build a modelling network that is oriented towards extracting as much value as possible from each interaction on and with the platform. Advertising—the main revenue stream for Zomato, since 2008—relies heavily on predictive models, to deliver hyper-targeted results on the basis of keywords, location, availability, rating, prices, etc. Data scientists have developed algorithms that improve the quality of images displayed on the app with the aim of increasing the click-through rate and, therefore, refining advertising strategies even further. In this respect, Zomato has taken up much of the Google model: a platform that starts by offering free information and services, conquers a large proportion of users and data, and then monetises this through tailored advertising and other for-a-fee services. Similar to Google, Zomato has leveraged the huge amount of data, accumulated in its ten years of operation, to add layers of services, gain control of the entire supply chain, and manage restaurants—including bookings, online ordering, and food supply—throughout the platform.

In New Town, restaurant owners have grown increasingly sceptical of the app and its hidden strategies. In 2015, I had the chance to speak with several restaurant owners in the area that regularly came up on the Zomato app. Back then, the platform had been active for four years already, but was still perceived as a relative novelty. Two restaurant owners in particular, MA and SC, were very collaborative and happy to share their thoughts with me, on a few occasions, after lunch service was over. Both their restaurants were located in New Town shopping malls—the heart of middle-class social life—and were eager to attract the young professionals working in the area and their families, as well as the business people that visited New Town for meetings and other engagements. In our conversations they generally expressed enthusiasm about the new digital showcase provided by Zomato; they felt as if they had more visibility, and more opportunities to attract new clients through deals, promotions, reviews, and pictures. More interestingly, both M and S repeatedly expressed the feeling that their relationship with the Zomato platform was one of equal terms and mutual convenience. By joining the app, they felt they were taking part in a horizontal network; somehow sharing their work and improvements and helping each other (Interview 21, 2015). It is important to remember that at the time of these conversations, Zomato was basically still a restaurant aggregator—an app that would find you a place to eat based on location, time of the day, type of food, and customers' reviews. In 2018, their perspective was considerably different. Because the platform's core business—at least in India—had shifted to food delivery and Gold membership, the app was no longer seen as a partner in a relationship of mutual opportunities, but as some kind of parasite. In the words of M: 'You can't stay out of it, or you are invisible; but if you are in, you have to work twice to keep up' (Personal conversation 6, March 2018). M mentioned the fast pace of work imposed by food delivery, the ever-present threat of bad reviews or obscuration on the platform, and the complimentary food and drinks that Zomato's Gold members were entitled to. The feelings of horizontality and mutuality had been replaced by a clear perception of the asymmetry of capital and computing power. The initial cooperation (albeit real or perceived) between the platform and its partners has evolved into a one-way extractive relationship.

Zomato echoes much of the Uber methods of labour management in its delivery component. Online forums, such as Quora and job search engines such as Indeed.com—where workers rate their employers and share their experiences—open a window onto the working conditions of Zomato riders. Riders are legally classified as independent partners, are paid piecework, and bear all the costs for fuel and vehicle maintenance. Formally, they are free to work as much or as little as they want, but many report that they are in fact expected to log in the app (that is, to work) for at least 50 hours per week and 25 hours during the weekend. Those who fail to comply with this unwritten rule, commonly face some sort of consequence, ranging from a 'motivational speech' (or scolding) from their supervisors to an algorithmic punishment, such as being assigned fewer deliveries. Orders and bonuses depend on performance, and a 'good performance' consists of being fast and not getting complaints from customers. The algorithms that are entrusted to optimise delivery are, in fact, designed to exploit the workforce to the full, by imposing delivery time, routes, daily targets, and ratings. The costs that Zomato and customers save on delivery are actually borne by a fleet of precarious workers, who are continually pushed to go faster and without complaints. The working conditions of Zomato riders are far from an isolated case. They reflect the patterns of labour exploitation imposed by food delivery platforms such as Foodora, Just Eat, and Deliveroo, in many cities around the world. Ugo Rossi (2019) documented the struggles and strategies of resistance of a group of bikers working for the German platform, Foodora, in Turin, Italy. In 2016, Foodora bikers went on a spontaneous strike, reclaiming less vexing working conditions and exposing the predatory strategies of their platform employer. In August and September 2019, Zomato riders started a protest in many cities across India, including Kolkata, as the company increasingly cut incentives, forcing delivery staff to work much longer shifts to earn the same amount of money. Much interestingly, in Howrah (near Kolkata), the protest brought together Hindu and Muslim workers complaining about being forced to deliver food against their religious beliefs—respectively, beef for the Hindus and pork for the Muslims. This happened at a time when tensions between Hindu and Muslim communities across India had been rising for years, and fuelled in particular by the divisive politics of the ruling Hindu party, BJP. In response to the protest, Zomato explained that it would be impossible to factor these kinds of religious preferences into the software that runs delivery logistics. This episode is at once illustrative of the violence of algorithmic management, and of its limits. If the algorithms remain impermeable to the workers claim, some contingencies and subjective trajectories can never be completely anticipated. While the platform continuously refines techniques to discipline and maximise the surplus extracted from the bodies and minds of workers, challenges to corporate command might come from improbable alliances on unexpected terrains, such as Hindu riders going on strike alongside their Muslim 'brothers' to defend each other's religious beliefs, and their common rights as workers (Srinivasan, 2019).

Zomato also features a social network style section, where 'foodies' share their experiences, and follow each other. This supply of spontaneous self-profiling is of great value to the platform. Users are encouraged to share their thoughts and pictures, and 'experts'—users who have posted several reviews and gained many followers—are rewarded with discounts, free meals, and invitations to private events. The more users interact, the better are analytics able to customise ads and promotions, and to refine predictive models. To make this flood of data productive, some policing is required. Users' content and behavioural patterns are analysed by an algorithm that is specifically designed to detect biased reviews and spam, so as to preserve the trustworthiness of the app, on which the entire advertising business depends. Foodie profiles are assigned a (hidden) credibility score, which affects their visibility and weight on the platform (Ruchikanarang, 2017). At the same time, active users represent a continuous supply of free labour to Zomato. As it is the case with Facebook and other social networks, the platform is literally built by user-generated content—pictures, posts, comments, reviews, etc.—which means time, thoughts, emotions, and energy. Moreover, users (often unwittingly) train and test new machine learning applications every time they give feedback on the content displayed, thus saving the platform considerable amounts of money. These forms of digital labour (Terranova, 2000, 2012), on which tech companies capitalise heavily, are obviously not remunerated. Machine learning turns opinions, emotions, and the mutual trust between users in the platform, into actionable information for advertising and marketing purposes.

The example of Zomato makes it clear how platforms speculate on urbanites and urban life. Platforms leverage urban habits and socio-spatial formations, such as something as ordinary as restaurants, to collect as much data as possible, by disseminating techniques of identification, monitoring, and profiling. On top of that, a set of ever-evolving algorithmic strategies seek to extract as much value as possible from the collected data by projecting future performances, needs, or desires. Data scientists, such as the Zomato teams, have embraced the performative power of analytics and are eager to push techniques that predict the tastes, cravings, and plans of users, or that put pressure on delivery riders in order to increasingly reduce logistics costs, even forward. As seen earlier in this chapter, techniques that actively seek to induce, prevent, or affect actions, through a combination of data and sensing devices, can be described as examples of behavioural or synaptic manipulation (Degli Esposti, 2014; Halpern et al. 2013). One might argue that if this has always been the goal of the advertising industry, contemporary technology has the potential to bring these conditioning strategies to an unprecedented depth and ubiquity. And within the contemporary organisation of production under biocognitive capitalism, life as a whole—from our biological and reproductive features to our cognitive capabilities—is inscribed in the process of valorisation, far beyond the boundaries of formal working time, contracts, and salary. Today, big data and analytics seem capable of accomplishing this tendency as never before. Where Uber drivers drive themselves to sleep deprivation, to see their score rising on the app, or when Zomato users spend their off-work time writing reviews, in the hope of getting discounts, data extractivism shows all of its material grip on life, and the forms of corporeal exploitation it relies on. After these examples, the idea that smart cities are trying to craft 'a new form of life that is itself the product' (Halpern et al., 2013, p. 290) gets more grip. Only the testbed is not just Songdo, but every city that is experimenting with ubiquitous computation.

SPECULATION AND EXTRACTION BEYOND SURVEILLANCE

In the wake of the rise of data-driven platforms, sociologist, Shoshana Zuboff (2015, 2019) has famously proposed the notion of surveillance capitalism. Taking the business and computational architecture of Google as a leading example, Zuboff defines surveillance capitalism as a 'new logic of accumulation' and argues that a 'new form of information capitalism aims to predict and modify human behaviour as a means to produce revenue and market control' (2015, p. 75). This has become possible because of the expansion of a 'ubiquitous networked institutional regime that records, modifies and commodifies everyday experience from toasters to bodies, communication to thought, all with a view to establishing new pathways to monetisation and profit' (p. 81). Zuboff calls this architecture *Big Other*, and suggests that it blurs the boundaries between private and public, enforcing a new form of 'instrumentarian' power that exceeds the state and the rule of law. For Zuboff, the 'behavioural surplus' extracted through pervasive dataveillance and the manipulation of users is a new frontier of value extraction and the crucial element that differentiates surveillance capitalism from previous forms of accumulation and valorisation (2019). In an extended review of Zuboff's latest book, *The Age of Surveillance Capitalism*, Evgeny Morozov (2019) criticises surveillance capitalism as a self-explanatory paradigm, which ultimately fails to account for how value is actually generated in the digital economy. Morozov maintains that surveillance and behavioural manipulation, if they exist at all, are only subordinate to the evergreen capitalist strategy of appropriating surplus and dominating the market. Among the many criticisms that Morozov raises to Zuboff's theory, the most relevant here is that the idea of behavioural surplus explains only a limited portion of contemporary value extraction. For Morozov, the idea of behavioural surplus overlooks other forms of extraction in the 'digitized social factory' that are by no means less predatory. This point is particularly relevant to the discussion of urban extractivism in this chapter. As the last few pages have illustrated, behavioural manipulation via algorithms definitely exists, and it is engineered (or at least, deliberately attempted) by commercial platforms at many levels. Yet, I depart from Zuboff's analysis for two major reasons. First, I argue that behavioural surplus is not only extracted through advertising (as Zuboff seems to suggest) but also from the algorithmic disciplining of labour (see Uber) and free labour (AI training and UGC, see Zomato). Second, I suggest that these forms of surplus are only possible because of a planet-wide chain of extraction, which connects mining sites, hedge funds, tech startups, and urban gentrification, the materiality of which is missing from Zuboff's advertising-focused analysis.

In his long piece on *The Baffler*, Morozov painstakingly dissects the shortcomings and weaknesses of Zuboff's arguments, mostly the emphasis on technological innovations and failure to grasp capitalism structural dynamics. Yet this critique does not, in my view, go much farther than Zuboff's. In essence, Morozov counters the analytical framework of surveillance capitalism with the argument of 'capitalism as usual'. The issue of behavioural manipulation is dismissed as something that has always been endemic to capitalism and that is not very different today from what happened during the neoliberal turn of the 1980s. This might be true, but does not exempt us from addressing the specific forms wherein the conditioning of attention and affects is unfolding today, and the implications of this conditioning in terms of value extraction. Throughout the essay, Morozov plays structural capitalist dynamics—such as keeping costs low, growing faster than competitors, using political power to gain favourable regulations, and ensuring long-term profitability—off against the (minor, for Morozov) 'novelty' of value extraction from behavioural manipulation. What I find more problematic in Zuboff's framework, and that falls outside Morozov's concerns, is in fact how the relationship between surveillance and value extraction is conceptualised. Surveillance capitalism has the merit of drawing attention to the ways in which algorithmic tools are leveraged to create value, too similar to the ways in which they are used for security purposes. Data are captured and sold to advertisers, data brokers, and other companies; users generate information that is monetised, in a form of labour that is not acknowledged, let alone remunerated; and access to deeply personal and intimate information (including, for example, fitness and sleep trackers or fertility apps) may result into punitive policies or attempts to manipulate behaviour through hyper-targeted advertising. In other words, surveillance capitalism hints at the disturbing nexus between security and economy, which is delineating as modelling becomes a far too popular technique of doing things. Yet, as is common when surveillance is the vantage point, what happens between watching and data capture, and their outputs, that is, the techniques that turn data into actionable information and therefore value, remains overlooked. Earlier in this book, I have shown how smart cities are inscribed within a grid of preemptive models. This calculative framework links government and commercial operations and blurs the borders between security and value extraction. It is not just that the methods employed to make security decisions or money are the same; or that the technology providers are the same; but rather the fact that the logic informing urban security platforms and capitalist platforms—a possibilistic, speculative logic of anticipation and preemption—is the same. The EPIC platform in Cape Town and the Uber platform in New Town are obviously different in content and scale, but not in their operational logic. Both platforms try to anticipate events and to make them actionable in the present. The Xpresso analytics for social media content, tested in New Town Kolkata for urban security, was originally created and commercialised for marketing and customer management. The models used for predicting markets or for measuring urban policies, are formally identical. I do not mean to suggest that either field has taken control of the other. To quote Louise Amoore once more, it is neither "the securitisation of the economy," nor "the privatisation of security" (2013, p. 54) that we see here. Nor, I add, is it surveillance. Rather, it is a technical and logical shift towards speculation that informs the algorithmic tools in the first place and articulates strategies of both government and value extraction accordingly. This leads us to discussing how speculation and extraction are articulated in the urban operations of platforms. The remainder of this chapter illustrates how speculation and extraction coexist, overlapping and feeding each other by continually stretching the boundaries of present and future. Speculative calculations draw possible futures in the present, in the form of predictive models, e.g.

risk alerts, customised ads, price surges, discount offers, etc. At the same time, urban extractivism takes many forms, digital and non-digital, which are prompted by, and prompt in turn, a calculus of the future (even when that suture is extremely close, as in now-casting).

From land grabbing in the establishment of Special Economic Zones, to gentrification driven by venture capital in the tech sector, the examples reviewed earlier in this chapter connect to debates on speculative urbanism (Goldman, 2011; Fields, 2023; Leitner & Sheppard, 2023) showing how financial and real estate circuits are mobilised in smart city making. At the same time, by bringing the focus on platforms like Uber and Zomato, and on the role of speculative algorithmic technologies in extracting value from workers, customers, and the urban environment, I point to yet another fold of speculative urbanism. Land grabbing for Special Economic Zones in New Town Kolkata fits within what Goldman (2011) describes as 'speculative geographies', where cities are transformed into spaces of accumulation through large-scale land acquisitions, and urban space is reconfigured to accommodate home-grown and global capital at the expenses of local communities. What happened in Rajarhat resonates with Goldman's (2011) work on speculative urbanisation in Bangalore. Both cities have been positioned as sites of potential economic growth under the banner of technology and innovation, but their transformation is largely driven by chains of local and capital investments, aiming to capture future rent or sale profits. In this context, Special Economic Zones represent a 'territorial fix' for capital, where land is, often forcibly, repurposed for investors, continually repositioned as an asset to be bought, sold, and speculated upon. In parallel, the rise of Cape Town's startup ecosystem is not only a reflection of local entrepreneurialism, but also a byproduct of global financial flows that target specific economic and urban spaces as sites for investments. As Fields (2017) notes, financial capital is directly involved in the production of urban space, through the incessant movements of real estate and (re)development projects. The story of Woodstock's transformation is exemplar in this sense, insofar as housing and commercial properties have been turned into financial assets as part of broader narratives of urban smartness in the making. In this process, and despite its distance and abstraction from the city fabric (Fields, 2017), finance works in fact as a form of urban governance, dictating the functional and aesthetic reorganisation of spaces (Leitner et al., 2008).

While playing with the future, urban speculations are fuelled by the extraction of value from cities in the present. Rent and the valorisation of land and property are one crucial side of these extractive processes (Massuh, 2014, pp. 55–60, cited by Gago & Mezzadra, 2017, p. 580), which are deeply intertwined with speculative projects and visions of the smart city. But at the same time, broader forms of extraction are at work, to which the algorithmic architecture of platforms is key. As John Stehlin (2018) puts it, cities are 'the theatre of platform capitalism', where producers and consumers of digital products, capital, workforce, and infrastructure concentrate. By providing a digital intermediation of locally available services, such as car rides or meal delivery, platforms operate as infrastructures of rent extraction, which capture what Stehlin calls 'place-based value'. This definition of rent is obviously broader than landlord payments, pointing to the wealth of (datafied) urban environments, which is at stake in these economic formations. As Ugo Rossi puts it, platforms 'are interested in exploiting the commonwealth of metropolitan environments (in terms of codified and socially diffused knowledge, entrepreneurial life forms and relational abilities)' (2019, p. 1429). This is clear, for example, in the strategies that control and maximise the extraction of time and energy from the bodies of the workers, as seen in the interactions between Uber drivers, Zomato riders, and their algorithmic supervisors. At the same time, platforms create and maintain their products by appropriating the free labour users provide, for example, the creation of content, such as ratings and reviews, or training machine learning applications. Furthermore, the continuously fine-tuned predictive analytics seek to monetise and manipulate the users' emotions and attention, turning personal data into a customised offer of services. Algorithms and predictive models are also critical in linking extractive practices to financial speculation. As the cases of Uber and Zomato demonstrate, urban data are a key asset for operations that are backed and driven by financial projects. The more data platforms extract, the more they bet on its future value through anticipatory actions. Algorithms do not merely react to current conditions; they actively shape future possibilities by speculating on potential outcomes. Uber's use of surge pricing, for example, is a form of speculative pricing, where the platform anticipates future demand and adjusts prices accordingly to maximise margins. Zomato's use of machine learning models to optimise delivery times and customer preferences similarly reflects the attempt to generate a market for food delivery. And these operations are inscribed into global financial chains that include funding rounds, stakeholder politics, IPOs, and more. In conclusion, the urban operations of platform capitalism reveals a complex interplay of extraction, speculation, and value creation that extends far beyond traditional notions of rent. As cities transform into arenas of data-driven exploitation, the implications for labor, community, and the very fabric of urban life demand critical examination and collective resistance. Some ideas on the latter will be reviewed in the next, and final chapter of this book.

References

Acaroglu, L. (2013). *The secret life of unsustainable stuff: Designing the future of consumption.* TED Talk. Retrieved from https://www.ted.com/

Amoore, L. (2013). *The Politics of Possibility: Risk and Security Beyond Probability.* Duke University Press.

Bathia, R. (2018). The amazing way Zomato uses data science for success. *Analytics India Mag.* Retrieved on October 12, 2018 from https://analyticsindiamag.com/the-amazing-way-zomato-uses-data-science-for-success/

Chakraborty, S. & Gosh, D. (2018, October 31). App cab drivers call 2-day strike against firm's 'excess'. *Times of India.* Retrieved on December 10, 2018 from https://timesofindia.indiatimes.com/city/kolkata/app-cab-drivers-call-2-day

Couldry, N., & Mejias, U. A. (2018). *The costs of connection: How data is colonizing human life and appropriating it for capitalism.* Stanford University Press.

Crawford, K., & Joler, V. (2018). *Anatomy of an AI system: The Amazon Echo as an anatomical map of human labor, data, and planetary resources.* AI Now Institute. https://anatomyof.ai

De Greef, K. (2016, May 26). *Uber and out: Drivers in Cape Town are working 24-hour shifts for low pay.* GroundUp. Retrieved on March 3, 2017 from https://www.groundup.org.za/article/uber-and-out-drivers-cape-town-are-working-24-hour-shifts-low-pay/

Degli Esposti, S. (2014). When big data meets dataveillance: The hidden side of analytics. *Surveillance & Society, 12*(2), 209–225.

Dey, I., Samaddar, R., & Sen, S. K. (2013). *Beyond Kolkata: Rajarhat and the dystopia of urban imagination.* Routledge India.

Dhillon, A. (2018, December 4). My life is spent in this car': Uber drives its Indian workers to despair. *The Guardian.* Retrieved on Febryary 3, 2019 from https://www.theguardian.com/global-development/2018/dec/04/my-life-is-spent-in-this-car-uber-drives-indian-workers-to-despair

5 FROM LAND TO DATA: MONEY IN THE SMART CITY **145**

Fainstein, S. (2016). Financialisation and justice in the city: A commentary. *Urban Studies*, *53*(7), 1503–1508. https://www.jstor.org/stable/261 51126

Fields, D. (2017). Urban struggles with financialization: Rent, dispossession and the contested terrain of urban housing. *Geoforum*, *89*, 84–93. https://doi.org/10.1016/j.geoforum.2017.06.005

Fields, D. (2023). Speculative urbanism. *Environment and Planning A: Economy and Space*, *55*(2), 511–516.

Fumagalli, A. (2011). Twenty theses on contemporary capitalism (Cognitive capitalism and the financialization of bioeconomy). *Journal of the Theoretical Humanities*, *16*(3), 7–17.

Gago, V., & Mezzadra, S. (2017). A critique of the extractive operations of capital: Toward an expanded concept of extractivism. *Rethinking Marxism*, *29*(4), 574–591.

Goldman, M. (2011). Speculative urbanism and the making of the next world city. *International Journal of Urban and Regional Research*, *35*(3), 555–581.

Halbert, L., & Attuyer, K. (2016). The real estate/financial complex: Regional restructuring and urban governance in European cities. *Urban Studies*, *53*(7), 1517–1533.

Halpern, O., LeCavalier, J., Calvillo, N., & Pietsch, W. (2013). Test-bed urbanism. *Public Culture*, *25*(2 70), 272–306.

HIDCO. (2017). *HIDCO starts lottery for allotment of affordable housing*. Times of India. Retrieved from http://timesofindia.indiatimes.com

Interview 21. (June 2015). MA and SC, restaurant owners in New Town Kolkata [in person].

Kenney, M., & Zysman, J. (2019). The platform economy: Restructuring the space of capitalist accumulation. *Cambridge Journal of Regions, Economy and Society*, *13*(1), 55–76.

Lazzarato, M. (1997). Immaterial Labor. In P. Virno & M. Hardt (Eds.), *Radical Thought in Italy* (pp. 133–147). University of Minnesota Press.

Lazzarato, M. (2015). *Governing by debt*. Semiotext(e).

Lazonick, W. (2014). Profits without prosperity. *Harvard Business Review*, *92*(9), 46–55.

Leitner, H., & Sheppard, E. (2023). Unleashing speculative urbanism: Speculation and urban transformations. *Environment and Planning A*, *55*(2), 359–366.

Leitner, H., Sheppard, E., & Sziarto, K. M. (2008). The spatialities of contentious politics. *Transactions of the Institute of British Geographers*, *33*(2), 157–172.

Marazzi, C., Lebedeva, M., & Gimsey, E. (2011). *The violence of financial capitalism*. Semiotext(e).

146   I. ANTENUCCI

Massuh, G. (2014). *El derecho a la ciudad en el Siglo XXI*. Buenos Aires, Argentina: Siglo XXI Editores.

Mebelengwa, V. (2018, November 12). *Uber & Taxify shut down*. [Press release] https://twitter.com/SAEHA_SA_/status/1061996932283973634

Mezzadra, S., & Neilson, B. (2017). *The politics of operations: Excavating contemporary capitalism*. Duke University Press.

Morini, C., & Fumagalli, A. (2010). Life put to work: Towards a life theory of value. *Ephemera: Theory & Politics in Organization, 10*(3/4), 234–252.

Morozov, E. (2017). *Digital intermediation of everything: At the intersection of politics, technology and finance*. https://rm.coe.int/digital-intermediation-of-everything-at-the-intersection-of-politics-t/168075baba

Morozov, E. (2019, February 4). Capitalism's new clothes. *The baffler*. Retrieved on September 1, 2019, from https://thebaffler.com/latest/capitalisms-new-clothes-morozov

Mosco, V. (2015). *To the cloud: Big data in a turbulent World*. Paradigm Publishers.

Munn, L. (2017). I am a driver–partner. *Work Organisation, Labour & Globalisation, 11*(2), 7–20.

O'Neill, C. (2016). *Weapons of math destruction: How big data increases inequality and threatens democracy*. Crown Publishing.

Personal conversation 4. (May 2015). RC, real estate executive, New Town [in person]

Personal conversation 5. (October 2022). RC, real estate executive, New Town [online]

Personal conversation 6. (March 2018). MA and SC, restaurant owners in New Town Kolkata [online].

Pollio, A. (2019).) Forefronts of the sharing economy: Uber in Cape Town. *International Journal of Urban and Regional Research, 43*(4), 760–775.

Rossi, U. (2019). The common-seekers: Capturing and reclaiming value in the platform metropolis. *Environment and Planning c: Politics and Space, 37*(8), 1418–1433.

Rossiter, N. (2016). *Software, infrastructure, labor: A media theory of logistical nightmares*. Routledge.

Rouanet, H., & Halbert, L. (2016). Leveraging finance capital: Urban change and self-empowerment of real estate developers in India. *Urban Studies, 53*(7), 1401–1423. https://www.jstor.org/stable/26151121

Ruchikanarang. (2017, February 13). With great power comes great responsibility [Blog post]. https://www.zomato.com/blog/with-great-power-comes-great-responsibility

Smart City Proposal Annexures for New Town, Kolkata. (n.d.) http://164.100.161.224/upload/uploadfiles/files/Annexures_Kolkata.pdf

Sadowski, J. (2019). When data is capital: Datafication, accumulation, and extraction. *Big Data & Society,* 6(1). https://doi.org/10.1177/2053951718820549

SAVCA (South African Venture Capital and Private Equity Association). (2017). *Private equity industry survey of South Africa.* Retrieved from https://savca.co.za/research-reports/

Schlanger, Z. (2018, April 17). If shipping were a country, it would be the sixth-biggest greenhouse gas emitter. *Quartz.* Retrieved on September 16, 2019 from https://qz.com/1253874/if-shipping-were-a-country-it-would-the-worlds-sixth-biggest-greenhouse-gas-emitter/

Srinivasan, C. (2019, August 12). *"Forced to deliver beef and pork": Zomato riders protest in Howrah.* NDTV. Retrieved on February 28, 2020 from https://www.ndtv.com/india-news/forcing-us-to-deliver-beef-and-pork-say-zomato-riders-in-kolkata-2083632

Srivastava, S. (2018, April 3). Brookfield is reaping the rewards of its patiently deployed capital. *Forbes India.* Retrieved on July 4, 2018 from http://www.forbesindia.com/article/real-estate-special-2018/brookfield-is-reaping-the-rewards-of-its-patiently-deployed-capital/49841/1

Srnicek, N. (2016). *Platform capitalism.* Polity Press.

Stehlin, J. (2018). *Cyclescapes of the unequal city: Bicycle infrastructure and uneven development.* University of Minnesota Press.

Terranova, T. (2000). Free labor: Producing culture for the digital economy. *Social Text,* 18(2), 33–58.

Terranova, T. (2012). *Network culture: Politics for the information age.* Pluto Press.

Uber. (2014, November 10). *Uber vehicle financing: Bringing entrepreneurship to the Indian. Grassroots* Retrieved on May 27, 2015 from https://www.uber.com/en-IN/blog/uber-vehicle-financing-bringing-entrepreneurship-to-the-indian-grassroots/

Uber. (2016, June 30). *Enabling entrepreneurship.* Retrieved on July 14, 2018, from https://www.uber.com/en-IN/blog/enabling-entrepreneurship/

Weber, R. (2010). Selling city futures: The financialization of urban redevelopment policy. *Economic Geography,* 86(3), 251–274.

Zomato buys Tech Eagle Innovations to work on drone—based food delivery. (2018, December 5). *Tech Economic Times India.* https://tech.economictimes.indiatimes.com/news/startups/zomato-buys-tech-eagle-innovations-to-work-on-drone-based-food-delivery/66951972

Zuboff, S. (2015). Big other: Surveillance capitalism and the prospects of an information civilization. *Journal of Information Technology, 30*(1), 75–89.

Zuboff, S. (2019). *The age of surveillance capitalism: The fight for a human future at the new frontier of power*. Profile Books.

CHAPTER 6

Beyond the Smart City: Speculating Otherwise

As a buzzword as well as a planning framework, the 'smart' city feels already as a thing of the past. Between the Covid-19 outbreak and the early 20s, the term has somehow lost its charm and has largely disappeared from media, policy, and academic outlets. Scholars have already started thinking 'beyond'[1] or 'after the smart city' (Launguillon-Aussel, 2024) and proposing categories to differentiate the phase of 'smart urbanism from the upcoming phase of AI urbanism' (Cugurullo et al., 2024). More than in drawing boundaries, however, I am interested in charting what smart cities have left behind, along with the heavy baggage of urban digital infrastructures. Smart cities might be dead indeed, but urban speculations are more alive than ever. Projects like Songdo, Halpern and colleagues write, (2013) have forged a new rationality and epistemology that is bound to pervasive computation, and affects the whole spectrum of urban life. Notions of time and space change radically, as every form of human and non-human interaction—from the use of natural resources to the education and medical conditions of residents—is recast through data and analytics. What is being tested in Songdo, and digital cities projects at large, is a vision of technological self-government; one in which the future is made completely calculable, and the balancing of risks and

---

[1] See for instance the 'Beyond Smart Cities Today: Power, Justice and Resistance' Conference, which took place in Malmö, 16–17 June 2022.

© The Author(s), under exclusive license to Springer Nature Switzerland AG 2025
I. Antenucci, *Future-proofed*,
https://doi.org/10.1007/978-3-031-86429-2_6

149

opportunities can be achieved through algorithms. Not insignificantly, these predictions collapse into production, since Songdo is also among the largest real estate projects in the world, and the entire system that is being tested there is meant to be sold and reproduced. Songdo, and smart cities in general, are *testbeds*: sites where the experimentation of new computing infrastructures reconfigures, or seeks to, daily life, government, and value extraction. Halpern and colleagues have been criticised for emphasising dystopian corporate mega-projects of uncertain realisation, overlooking the more mundane and mixed fabric of the 'actually existing' smart cities (Shelton, Zoog & Wiig, 2015). Yet they have opened up an interpretative space that I believe sheds light on smart projects of any scale and size, by linking technological power, urban management, and commercial interests. The link is speculation: the effort to define and dictate the future that runs through infrastructures, governance, and urban economies.

The aim of this book was never to conduct a comparative study of two cities or to fulfil a multi-sited ethnographic agenda. What I tried to do instead is to present a form of urbanism that seeks to shape the future by governing the present, and to govern the present by appealing to the future. Powered and informed by the inner logic of computing technologies, this form of urbanism includes of course the more obvious form of speculations—the financial ones—but cannot be reduced to them. It rather illustrates the convergence of multiple ways—epistemic, planning, managerial, and commercial—of morphing and appropriating urban futures. I am not suggesting that there is one overarching paradigm of speculative urbanism at work on a global scale. Throughout this book, I have rather traced and charted the contingencies and sometimes unique genealogies through which speculative forces condense and unfold in urban environments.

So distant in many ways, both New Town Kolkata and Cape Town are nodes within planetary networks of technological experimentation, extraction, and circulation of capital. They have also been landing points of a global model of smart cities, which has been reworked and complicated by situated narratives, interests, and tensions. In both these cities, digitalisation is invested with a twofold significance, as an urban technology for development and (at least in Cape Town) social justice, and as a path for positioning among global circuits of capital. The New Town smart city and the 'Bengal Silicon valley' might well remain little more than an urban chimera; and Cape Town, in its race for regional tech leadership, might have already moved beyond the smart city framework. But whatever path the cities are going to take, the appetite for predicting, controlling, and monetising the future through data and algorithms is unlikely to disappear. The smart city experiments have sedimented infrastructures, business models, and ways of knowing and understanding the urban environment. As a result, urban speculations are proliferating, on the initiative of the private sector especially. Yet speculations, as conceptual tools, are not necessarily in service of discriminatory, oppressive, or exploitative forces: some of them, as we will see shortly, might open up alternatives for urban futures not bound to algorithmic governance and capitalist extraction. In the remainder of this final chapter, I will first recap the key findings of this book, making clear how cities are becoming more and more sites of speculative processes. I will then suggest two possible directions for further research on this theme. One concerns the evolution of platform urbanism, or how powerful platforms such as Amazon speculate on urban environments through pervasive machine learning technologies and in so doing, are de facto taking up functions of urban planning and governance. The second one looks at the flip side of speculation: at the ideas, suggestions, and provocations that do not accept urban futures of algorithmic oppression as already written, and speculate instead on futures of liberation and equality.

FUTURES

Smart cities are speculative worlds. At the core of their projects and experiments lies the aspiration to anticipate and somehow manage the future. As this book has shown, speculation runs through the projects and continuous tests which do not merely represent the future city, but drag it into the present and shape its trajectories by generating narratives, protocols, norms, and investments. Speculation runs through algorithms in the security and government platforms that incessantly model performances, behaviours, and events, enabling preemptive decisions. And it runs through the financial operations behind the proliferation of tech startups, the development of smart enclaves, and the growth of commercial platforms. If, as Lisa Adkins (2018) suggests, speculation is increasingly a logic of social organisation, then smart city projects have been laboratories where the possibilities and limits of this logic have been explored with particular intensity. Critical to these explorations, experiments, and tests is the exploitation of possible futures, for security or economic purposes. Extensively collected, data are then modelled into predictions and decisions. Models do not merely *represent* but *produce* specific futures. I have detailed how the algorithmic operations of both security and commercial platforms are designed to generate configurations of future possibilities that are actionable in the present for either governance or economic actions. As several studies have shown (Amoore, 2013; Aradau, 2015; Pasquinelli, 2017), these algorithmic operations are contingent, often self-referential, and strongly imaginative. The rules of association of algorithms follow a logic of resemblance and correspondence that are, as Aradau (2015) suggests, closer to divination than to scientific evidence. Models work through criteria of proximity, similarity, and sympathy, not discovering patterns, but creating them. However, the results they produce are highly performative in at least two ways: first, because they sort the city into normative categories that have material consequences; second, because these categories feed back into the data sets and thus become the basis for the next models. We have seen several examples of speculative mechanisms in action: risk alerts of crime incidents and criminal hot spots, scoring citizens for their access to social services and benefits, rating the performances of Uber drivers or delivery riders, profiling customers to anticipate their desires.

Looking at both security and commercial platforms, we have seen a convergence of techniques and operations. As Louise Amoore (2013) notes, following Deleuze and Guattari (1980), the relationship between government and economy is such that neither of them can be reduced to, or absorbed by, the other; rather, they resonate together and infiltrate each other in multiple ways, as they both play on the imagination and calculation of possible futures. As De Goede et al. (2014) phrase it, speculative security 'draws attention to the precise ways in which uncertain futures are commodified and is attentive to the tensions thus generated within commercial and professional practices' (p. 419). Security is increasingly driven by a logic of preemption which works 'in a way that mirrors speculative finance'. Like finance, preemption is not about predicting the future, but about 'acting on multiple possible futures by drawing them into the present as terrain of intervention' (p. 419). Speculative models of the urban future become the terrain where biopolitical interventions and strategies of value extraction come into play simultaneously, as they produce both actionable subjects and environments at the same time.

Speculative platforms seek to shape, mould, direct, or force the positioning of things and humans in time and space. This is more than surveillance or dataveillance: it is generative power, ontogenesis. The category of surveillance does not grasp the productive character of the algorithms at work in security platforms, which do not merely gather data, but also turn them into action. In parallel, the idea of surveillance capitalism (Zuboff, 2019) does not comprehend consider how platforms do not simply accumulate and sell information, but actively produce their own workers, markets, and consumers. Examples of two platforms like Uber and Zomato have made clear how a highly sophisticated and continuously tuned apparatus of data mining and algorithmic modelling operates, to continually maximise and expand the extraction of value from workers, users, and the whole urban environment. But I have also pointed to the nexus between such extractive practices and the circuits of financial speculations which allow platforms to emerge and grow. This hits the urban ground with particular violence: the creation of startup ecosystems and platform economies comes after, or along with, land grabbing and gentrification, dispossession and evictions. Not only individuals— workers or customers—but multiple forms of urban life, and the urban environment at large, are captured in these speculative processes.

THE BANALITY OF URBAN SPECULATIONS

The momentum of smart cities might be fading or faded already. Platforms, however, are here to stay. Over the past few years, literature has drawn attention to the many ways in which platforms are reconfiguring urban environments and governance beyond smart city policies, and the notion of *platform urbanism*, forged by Sarah Barns (2020), has become key across a number of disciplines, from media studies to urban and political geography. In recent work, Fran Meissner and I (2024) look at the ways in which AI technologies are unfolding in, and transforming, urban spaces from the angle of commercial platforms. These are often leading the urban deployment of AI infrastructures along with, or ahead of, government programmes. In this process, we argue that commercial platforms and their proprietary, profit-oriented technologies are increasingly reconfiguring urban environments, and taking up roles and functions that used to be, or theoretically still are, in the hands of public urban planning and governance. Private companies are generally far ahead public bodies in the research and development of AI technologies, and enlist cities both as markets and testbeds for new applications. These involve infrastructures and services that are becoming more and more essential to urban everyday life, such as logistics and security. As business operations move faster and more effectively than public policy and democratic deliberations, these transformations tend to bypass supervision and regulations. In other words, commercial AI infrastructures operate as technopolitical forces, which reconfigure not only the actors and forms of urban governance but their very political premises. How can we locate and scrutinise power, when critical decisions about the urban space are taken by black-boxed algorithms, designed to generate profits for business platforms? What space remains for accountability and democratic processes, when urban infrastructures are controlled by machine learning systems, which set their own rules of knowledge and produce their own norms (Amoore, 2022)?

A striking example of these issues comes from Amazon, as recent work done with my colleagues Armin Beverungen, Maja-Lee Voigt, and Klara Friese (forthcoming), proposes. With a clear strategy of expansion across different market segments, and ramifications ranging from the e-commerce of anything, to logistics, security, entertainment, and of course, advanced research in AI to support all of the above, Amazon is in a unique position to exert its influence in and over urban environments. And if it is true that Amazon's business model and operations take place globally and at multiple scales, nevertheless cities are strategic nodes both for testing and implementing specific technologies, protocols and products. Take for example Amazon's massive apparatus of supply, stocking, and delivery—in a word, logistics. Not everyone might find it obvious to think of it as a speculative infrastructure. Yet the incessant operations of warehouses, trucks, and vans are in fact orchestrated by machine learning systems that seek to predict demand, anticipate shipping, and induce customers from a specific urban cluster to buy something at some point of time. In so doing, Amazon's algorithms model specific urban futures, which suit the company's goal to optimise logistics. But at the same time, these speculations impact upon the urban real estate market, circulation and pollution, local retail, and everyday habits. Land value goes up or down because of proximity to warehouses. Delivery vehicles add to already congested traffic, and related CO_2 emissions. More people buy groceries online and local shops shut down. This is one dimension of what we propose to look at as Amazon's urbanism: the growing power of Amazon in/over cities, and the ways in which it is creating, or destroying, urban worlds. But there is more to it than logistics: as Amazon expands into new market segments, such as security or IoT appliances, its speculations multiply and its infrastructural power rises.

With Ring technologies for AI home security, which include 'smart' devices for home surveillance as well as Neighbors, a social media for Ring users, Amazon is actively speculating on racist and class anxieties in US neighbourhoods. Extensively distributed across American households, Ring devices generate risk alerts for 'suspicious' activities, which are then shared and magnified on social media. In this process, critics have noticed how seemingly innocuous activities are discursively framed as security threats and trigger aggressive reactions, often with a racist tone. By partnering with local law enforcement agencies, while feeding a culture of paranoia, surveillance, and over-reaction, Amazon Ring is reconfiguring how urban security is perceived and organised. In a context where racism is a long-standing feature, and urban inequalities are on the rise, the new security paradigm enabled by Ring is likely to exacerbate discriminatory behaviours, and it has already made some victims. As Lauren Bridges (2021) observes, through its seemingly benign security devices Amazon is in fact building and disseminating a carceral infrastructure across American suburbs. Another critical example of Amazon urbanism is Sidewalk, one of Amazon's most recent projects for IoT infrastructures. It is a protocol for a shared network that uses Bluetooth and LoRa technologies to extend the range of low-bandwidth devices, originally developed by startup Iotera, which Amazon acquired along with Ring in 2018. Amazon devices such as Echo or Ring can serve as bridges, providing connectivity to other compatible devices. Sidewalk officially launched in 2021 in the US and in 2023 it was opened to developers of compatible devices. According to a map released by Amazon, as of 2023 Sidewalk reached more than 90% of the US population[1]. Sidewalk integrates all sorts of trackers, sensors, and controllers for managing virtually anything, from home appliances to neighbourhood infrastructures. As the list of compatible devices is potentially endless, Sidewalk can make neighbourhoods almost fully automated, and locked in with Amazon's proprietary infrastructures. By creating an ecosystem of shared networks and connected services, Amazon acquires an infinite pool of data for profiling and modelling users' behaviours. With Sidewalk, Amazon has the chance to raise the game of algorithmic engineering, anticipating and steering habits, needs, and desires of entire neighbourhoods. This is clearly a remarkable business opportunity, but again, the effects of these technologies go beyond commerce. By taking over, or even turning into urban infrastructures, Amazon is, as Emily West (2022) puts it, becoming the very *background* of our everyday life, as well as, I

156   I. ANTENUCCI

would add, its *backbone*. As it becomes indispensable for more and more people, Amazon speculates on specific forms of urbanism and urbanity, where neighbourhood communities turn into proprietary, consumption-based, IoT-mediated ecosystems; and where the algorithmic modelling of consumption turns into a mode of urban governance.

Amazon is a compelling and sinister example of speculations *on* and *in* the urban space, where economic strategies fuse with the power of infrastructures in resetting the rules of space and living. But it is not the only one. Speculations on and in the city are not merely a prerogative of large, powerful platforms. Quite the contrary, speculation has become a mode of thinking, governing, and being in the city that runs through a myriad of actors and practices. The idea that future risks and opportunities can be modelled and acted upon is crucial to a broad spectrum of urban operations. Think of the routing apps that everyone uses, digital twins for architecture and planning, software that calculates housing needs and allocations, predictive policing, and more. Speculation becomes ordinary, even banal, and easily works as a form of mundane governance, as predictions and manipulations of the future become engrained in a plethora of everyday objects and practices.

Other Speculations: The Right to the AI City?

As AI technologies become more powerful and pervasive, are urban futures already written? Are they bound to manipulative algorithmic power, or can different trajectories be drawn? This book has presented readers with a long list of disquieting examples, controversies, and dangers. This does not mean, of course, that the speculative forces I described have gone completely unchallenged. In both Kolkata and Cape Town there have been strikes, anti-eviction movements, and campaigns for access to infrastructures and services, some of which have been mentioned in the previous chapters. In all these cases, understandably, people were fighting against the tangible effects of technological and financial speculations combined: lower salaries and poor working conditions, unaffordable rent and evictions, costs of services beyond control, and so on. At the same time, they were trying to physically identify and humanise their counterparts as much as possible. Uber drivers on strike sought negotiations with some human company officers. Obviously, nobody marched against predictive analytics, geolocators, or behavioural profiling. As cities become more digital and platformised, they increasingly operate as large-scale black boxes, where urban life, in all its forms, is increasingly governed and monetised by speculative models, through rules and criteria that are inscrutable for most of the population. What then, are the spaces and strategies for politics? To answer this question we need to go back to the notion of speculation itself. So far, this book has erred on the dark side of it, the one concerned with appropriating and colonising the future. But the notion holds an inherent ambivalence, and is also open to utopias, heterotopias, and radical visions of the future. As Wilkie, Savransky, and Rosengarten (2017) argue, speculation needs to be reclaimed from financial and security practices, and put to work to cultivate different possibilities. To conclude this book, I want to present some of these counter/alternative speculations on the city to be.

In the wake of smart urbanisation, Henri Lefebvre's idea of 'the right to city' has been revisited to face the new urban conditions and challenges of digitalisation. For Lefebvre, the right to the city consisted of a set of claims through which urban dwellers were able to take part in and shape urban processes, based on their needs and desires, rather than their being merely passive elements in the capitalist-driven dynamics of speculation and profit extraction. Michiel De Lange and Martjin de Waal (2013) expand on this idea, suggesting that 'the right to the digital city' is in the first place a right of appropriation that redefines the forms of ownership of technologies and infrastructures. The right to the digital city challenges privatisation and enables communities to share and make decisions about the use of smart resources and data. In their discussion of the informational rights to the city, Joe Shaw and Mark Graham (2017) focus on the methods through which data are collected, organised, and made available by tech giants such as Google, and on the political relevance of a digital representation of the urban space. Because only a few monopolists control this information, Shaw and Graham argue, it is imperative to imagine ways in which citizens can reclaim the production of urban information as part of 'sustained autogestion' (Shaw & Graham, 2017, p. 921). Evgeny Morozov and Francesca Bria (2018) link the right to the city to a proposal of urban technological sovereignty. That means defining legal and economic regimes for the collection and use of data and for the management of smart infrastructure, which are oriented to serve and empower local residents, rather than tech corporations or neoliberal urban governance. As an example of this proposal, a framework for technological sovereignty has been partially implemented in Barcelona under the administration of Mayor Ada Colau (Monge et al., 2022).

All of these interventions propose alternative forms of organisation of digital technologies in urban environments. Yet all of them focus, in one way or another, on the outer layer of algorithmic power. Transparency, collective ownership, and technological sovereignty pertain indeed to the legal and policy arrangements connecting urban technologies and urban dwellers. However, this book has illustrated how the socio-economic relations within which technologies unfold—who controls the algorithms, and the economic or political agenda in which they operate—are indissociable from the inner logic of algorithms, the rules they set and follow, the forms of knowledge and action they make possible. In other words, when it comes to algorithmic, or AI, power, the (potential) alternative must go beyond privacy, transparency, and public/collective management. We need to address their ontogenetic potential, that is, how they make, or break, worlds. The ways in which algorithms are designed, trained, tested, supervised, and updated, matters. This leads to very technical questions, such as on what datasets are the algorithms trained? How are data prepared and cleaned up, and what is left out of computation? What are the exact rules of association in use, and how is their effectiveness measured? How is unsupervised machine learning kept under control and evaluated? How do we critically compare the models with their living counterparts? Building on a body of critical work (among others, Apprich et al., 2018; Boyd & Crawford, 2012; Amoore, 2013; Aradau, 2015; Pasquinelli, 2017), in Chapter 3 of this book I drew attention to the critical aspects—the ways in which data are cleaned up and prepared; the fact that algorithmic speculations are presented and employed as predictions; the bias and flaws that become embedded and automated into procedures—that shape the operations of platforms. But more ethical and political questions are on the line. How can we trust algorithmic decisions? How can we balance speculative models with other forms of embodied, non-calculative knowledge? How is the chain of decisions that connects sensors, algorithms, and humans organised? Having engaged with some of these questions, Shintaro Miyazaki (2019) concluded with an invitation to collectively 'Take back the Algorithms'. Echoing the idea to 'take back the economy' advanced by J.K. Gibson-Graham and their colleagues (2013), the core of Miyazaki's proposal is to make algorithms more affordable in the sense of *commonisation*—something that is shared and cared for among communities. Here, 'making affordable', refers to various levels of action, including making algorithms more open and transparent, subtracting them from the control of tech capitalists and the dictates of immediate efficacy and profit, opening up potential alternatives through code-bending, and un-making their capitalist value. In essence, Miyazaki says that 'making affordable, in this context, means to liberate such systems from the constraints of fully predetermined "mastery," and instead enable users to become independent agents in their interactions with the systems in question' (2019, p. 274). Utopistic as it may sound, the idea of commonistic algorithms signals a pathway for rethinking our collective relations with computing infrastructures. Yet this also entails facing the actual geometries of power in which algorithms are immersed. In today's world, reclaiming algorithms from the grip of capital on a large scale equates to a comprehensive reorganisation of economic and social relations—a radical change, or even a revolution. Something that is difficult to imagine as a smooth, peaceful transition. Anyway, some hypotheses and experiments for autonomous organisations of and with algorithmic technologies have emerged over the past decade. In 2014, for example, Robert Gehl proposed a manifesto for socialised media, that is, systems of social networking that are alternatives to the monopoly of Facebook, Twitter, Google, etc. Built through collaborative work between experts and 'common users', Gehl's social media run on decentralised, horizontal architectures and free hardware, operate in a regime of copyleft, and (un)archive data in modalities that undermine any form of monetisation and surveillance. In parallel, the SenseLab in Montreal and the Economic Space Agency experimented with the development of alternative cryptocurrencies, to support the processes of collective creation and to contribute to building postcapitalist economic networks (Senselab 3EI, n.d.; Virtanen, 2019; Massumi, 2018). Building on Autonomist Marxist theory, Tiziana Terranova (2014) has repurposed Benjamin Bratton's (2016) idea of the stack of digital infrastructures as a new nomos of the earth, into the speculative proposal of a 'red stack': a new infrastructure for the 'common', which includes radically different relationships with, and appropriation of, money, social networks, and bio-hypermedia.[2] The red stack is a 'process of re-coding network

---

[2] 'Bio-hypermedia' was first used by Giorgio Griziotti (2014) to define 'the ever more intimate relation between bodies and devices which is part of the diffusion of smartphones, tablet computers and ubiquitous computation' (2014, para. 6).

architectures and information technologies, based on values other than exchange and speculation' (para. 7), where what are now largely infrastructures of algorithmic capitalism and control—cryptocurrencies, social networks, wearables, smart devices, and apps—are turned into forms of cooperation and redistribution of wealth and power.

As Louise Amoore (2020) has made clear, it is not only who or what algorithms serve, but also and especially how they think and render the world, that defines the battleground for alternatives in the age of machine learning. As Amoore writes, algorithms fabulate continuously, as they determine attributes, thresholds, and norms, ultimately making decisions about what counts or does not, what is seen or not, and what is normal or deviant. Bound to the production of usable outputs, these logics foreclose complexity and alternative futures. To resist and confront this, Amoore argues, it is necessary to embrace fabulations and to push them beyond their current boundaries, towards openness, hybridity, and undecidability. The same can be said for cities. As urban environments are more and more immersed in, and shaped by, AI technologies, claims for the defence of individual privacy or algorithmic transparency—whatever that means—sound like backward battles. As drawing boundaries between 'us' human citizens and our digital infrastructures becomes more and more difficult, how can we rather think different urban futures *with* and *through* algorithms? Without dismissing the fight for transforming technological power relations, I welcome Miyazaki's invitation to rethink cities 'more in solidarity with algorithms, which might be considered as something akin to companions or co-species' (2019, p. 280). We learn from feminist thinking to embrace hybrid ontologies and playful relationships with machines. And taking the ontogenetic power of technologies seriously, brighter urban futures can only come from new ways of *staying with* the algorithms, of creating and caring for a shared environment. This might look unlikely as long as technologies remain in the hands of capital and state power. But the directions and outcomes of ontogenesis are never pre-determined, and leave space for alternative ethics, experiments, and battles. Speculative thinking remains open, and so do urban futures.

References

Adkins, L. (2018). *The time of money*. Stanford University Press.

Amoore, L. (2022). Machine learning political orders. *Review of International Studies, 49*(1), 20–36. https://doi.org/10.1017/S0260210522000031

6 BEYOND THE SMART CITY: SPECULATING OTHERWISE   161

Amoore, L. (2013). *The politics of possibility: Risk and security beyond probability.* Duke University Press.

Amoore, L. (2020). *Cloud ethics: Algorithms and the attributes of ourselves and others.* Duke University Press.

Antenucci, I., & Meissner, F. (2024). AI and urban governance: From the perils of smart cities to Amazon Inc. urbanism. In R. Paul, E. Carmel, & J. Cobbe (Eds.), *Handbook on public policy and artificial intelligence* (pp. 423–434). Edward Elgar Publishing.

Antenucci, A., Beverungen, A., Freise, A., & Voigt, R. (forthcoming). *Amazon's urban speculations.*

Apprich, C., Chun, W. H. K., Cramer, F., & Steyerl, H. (2018). *Pattern discrimination.* Mattering Press.

Aradau, C. (2015). Crowded places are everywhere we go': Crowds, emergency, politics. *Theory, Culture & Society, 32*(2), 155–175.

Barns, S. (2020). *Platform urbanism: Negotiating platform ecosystems in connected cities.* Palgrave McMillan.

Boyd, D., & Crawford, K. (2012). Critical questions for big data: Provocations for a cultural, technological, and scholarly phenomenon. *Information, Communication & Society, 15*(5), 662–679.

Bratton, B. H. (2016). *The stack: On software and sovereignty.* MIT Press.

Bridges, L. (2021). Infrastructural obfuscation: Unpacking the carceral logics of the Ring surveillant assemblage. *Information, Communication & Society, 24*(6), 830–849. https://doi.org/10.1080/1369118X.2021.1909097

Cugurullo, F., Caprotti, F., Cook, M., Karvonen, A., M°Guirk, P., & Marvin, S. (2024). The rise of AI urbanism in post-smart cities: A critical commentary on urban artificial intelligence. *Urban Studies, 61*(6), 1168–1182. https://doi.org/10.1177/00420980231203386

de Goede, M., Simon, S., & Hojnik, M. (2014). Performing preemption. *Security Dialogue, 45*(5), 411–422.

Deleuze, G., & Guattari, F. (1980). *Mille plateaux.* Ed. de minuit.

Gehl, R. (2014). *Reverse engineering social media.* Temple University Press.

Gibson-Graham, J. K., Cameron, J., & Healy, S. (2013). *Take back the economy: An ethical guide for transforming our communities.* University of Minnesota Press.

Griziotti, G. (2014). Biorank: Algorithms and transformations in the bios of cognitive capitalism. *Quaderni di San Precario, 6.* http://quaderni.sanprecario.info/2014/02/biorank-algorithms-and-transformation-in-the-bios-of-cognitive-capitalism-di-giorgio-griziotti/

Halpern, O., LeCavalier, J., Calvillo, N., & Pietsch, W. (2013). Test-bed urbanism. *Public Culture, 25*(2), 272–306.

Halpern, O., LeCavalier, J., Calvillo, N., & Pietsch, W. (2015). Test-bed as urban epistemology. In S. Marvin, A. Luque-Alaya, & C. McFarlane (Eds.), *Smart urbanism: Utopian vision or false dawn?* (pp. 146–168). Routledge.

Kitchin, R., Cardullo, P., & Di Feliciantonio, C. (2018). Citizenship, justice and the right to the smart city. In R. Kitchin, P. Cardullo, & C. Di Feliciantonio (Eds.), *The right to the smart city* (pp. 1–26). Emerald Group Publishing.

De Lange, M., & De Waal, M. (2013). Owning the city: New media and citizen engagement in urban design. *First Monday, 18*(11) https://doi.org/10.5210/fm.v18i11.4954

Launguillon-Aussel, (2024). After the smart city. New urban issues and new generations of experimentations, stakeholders and technologies in Europe and Asia. [Call for Papers]. *Netcom.* https://journals.openedition.org/netcom/7331#toctoln1

Massumi, B. (2018). *99 theses on the revaluation of value: A postcapitalist manifesto.* University of Minnesota Press.

Miyazaki, S. (2019). Take back the algorithms! A media theory of commonistic affordance. *Media Theory, 3*(1), 269–286.

Monge, F., Barns, S., Kattel, R., & Bria, F. (2022). *A new data deal: The case of Barcelona.* UCL Institute for Innovation and Public Purpose. https://www.ucl.ac.uk/bartlett/publicpurpose/sites/bartlett_public_purpose/files/new_data_deal_barcelona_fernando_barns_kattel_and_bria_18_feb.pdf

Morozov, E., & Bria, F. (2018). *Rethinking the smart city.* Rosa Luxemburg Stiftung.

Pasquinelli, M. (2017). Machines that morph logic: Neural networks and the distorted automation of intelligence as statistical inference. *Glass Bead, 1*(1). https://www.glass-bead.org/article/machines-that-morph-logic/?lang=enview

Senselab 3EI. (n.d.). *3E process seed bank.* Retrieved on September 10, 2019 from https://www.senselab.ca/wp2/3e-process-seed-bank/

Shaw, J., & Graham, M. (2017). An informational right to the city? Code, content, control, and the urbanization of information. *Antipode, 49*(4), 907–927.

Shelton, T., Zook, M., & Wiig, A. (2015). The 'actually existing smart city.' *Cambridge Journal of Regions, Economy and Society, 8*(1), 13–25.

Terranova, T. (2014). Red stack attack. In R. Mackay and A. Avanessian (Eds.), *Accelerate: The accelerationist reader* (pp. 379–399). Urbanomic.

Virtanen, A. (2019, October 3). *Towards post-capitalism.* Medium. Retrieved on January 29, 2020 from https://medium.com/econaut/towards-post-capitalism-7679d2831408

West, E. (2022). *Buy now: How Amazon branded convenience and normalized monopoly.* MIT Press.

Wilkie, A., Savransky, M., & Rosengarten, M. (Eds.). (2017). *Speculative research: The lure of possible futures.* Routledge.

Zuboff, S. (2019). *The age of surveillance capitalism: The fight for a human future at the new frontier of power.* Profile Books.

List of Interviews and Personal Conversations

Interview 1. (May 2015). JS, NKT City manager, New Town [in person].

Interview 2. (December 2017). JS, NKT City manager [online].

Interview 3. (November 2017). MB, former intern at smart city consultancy firm in New Town [online].

Interview 4. (September 2016). PK. Female software engineer and leader of smart citizens group in New Town [online].

Interview 5. (November 2015). ZS, tech journalist and consultant, Cape Town [in person].

Interview 6. (November 2016). PDW, former city manager, Cape Town [in person].

Interview 7. (October 2018). MN, real estate analyst in Kolkata [online].

Interview 8. (November 2016). PV, former IT & development consultant, Cape Town. [in person].

Interview 9. (November 2016). KM, real estate operator, Cape Town [in person].

Interview 10. (November 2016). AG freelance tech journalist, Cape Town [in person].

Interview 11. (December 2016). MK, IT consultant, Cape Town [in person].

Interview 12. (May 2015). DB, City manager, New Town [in person].

© The Editor(s) (if applicable) and The Author(s), under exclusive license to Springer Nature Switzerland AG 2025
I. Antenucci, *Future-proofed*,
https://doi.org/10.1007/978-3-031-86429-2

166   LIST OF INTERVIEWS AND PERSONAL CONVERSATIONS

Interview 13. (March 2018). DB, City manager, New Town [Online].
Interview 14. (December 2021). DB, City manager, New Town [Online].
Interview 15. (June 2015). Smart City Consultant A, New Town Kolkata. [in person].
Interview 16. (June 2018). Smart City Consultant A. [Online].
Interview 17. (March 2023). Smart City Consultant A. [Online].
Interview 18. (June 2015). Smart City Consultant B, New Town Kolkata. [in person].
Interview 19. (March 2023). Smart City Consultant B. [online].
Interview 20. (February 2019). FK, IT and management analyst, Cape Town. [online].
Interview 21. (June 2015). MA and SC, restaurant owners in New Town Kolkata [in person].
Personal Conversation 1. (November 2018). AC, member of New Town Facebook Group [online].
Personal Conversation 2. (November 2018). AG, member of New Town Facebook Group [online].
Personal Conversation 3. (November 2018). RS, member of New Town Facebook Group [online].
Personal conversation 4. (May 2015). RC, real estate executive, New Town [in person].
Personal conversation 5. (October 2022). RC, real estate executive, New Town [online].
Personal conversation 6. (March 2018). MA and SC, restaurant owners in New Town Kolkata [online].

INDEX

A

Accelerate Cape Town, 17
Accenture, 15, 30, 117, 122, 125
Adkins, Lisa, 11, 151
advertising, 13, 20, 22, 32, 33, 42, 92, 118, 135, 138, 140, 141
Africa, 1, 3, 6, 9, 17, 21, 36, 37, 39, 46, 121, 124, 127
Agrawal, Rakesh, 119
algorithmic governance, 7, 151
algorithmic management, 81, 89, 120
algorithmic systems, 11, 85, 99, 103
Amazon, 22, 38, 46, 151, 154–156
Amoore, Louise, 10, 11, 85, 100, 103, 119, 152, 154, 158, 160
analytics, 10, 12, 62, 71, 84–87, 89, 91, 102, 105, 108, 124, 135, 138, 143, 149, 156
apartheid, 6, 9, 16, 37, 40, 90, 124
Aradau, Claudia, 10, 20, 85, 100, 103, 110, 152, 158
Asia, 3, 121, 123

B

Bandwidth Barn, 48
Banerjee, Mamata, 27, 31, 33, 41–44, 52, 123
Bayesian inferences, 10, 103
Bengal Silicon Valley, 1, 8, 29, 41–44, 46, 51, 52, 123, 126
Benjamin, Ruha, 10, 90, 159
Bharatiya Janata Party (BJP), 5
biased, 10, 101, 109, 138
big data, 3, 4, 8, 96, 97, 139
biocognitive capitalism, 120, 139
bordering, 9
broadband fibre, 1, 17, 38
Bulkeley, Harriet, 63, 64, 74

C

Chatterjee, Partha, 14, 44
Cirolia, Liza Rose, 3, 32, 38, 47, 48
Cisco, 5, 15, 28, 30
City of Cape Town, 6, 17, 36, 38, 39, 46, 47, 59, 63, 66, 71, 73, 75, 83, 106

© The Editor(s) (if applicable) and The Author(s), under exclusive license to Springer Nature Switzerland AG 2025
I. Antenucci, *Future-proofed*,
https://doi.org/10.1007/978-3-031-86429-2

168 INDEX

class, 6, 8, 10, 14, 16, 22, 30, 34, 44, 45, 49, 52, 68, 76, 78, 89, 91, 93, 95, 103, 124, 128, 129, 135, 155
cloud computing, 38, 46
colonialism
colonial, 6, 120
colonial urbanism, 14
Columbia University, 5
corporate power, 3
Couldry, Nick, 120, 121
COVID-19, 2, 42, 66, 67, 149

D

data centres, 38
data extractivism, 118, 120, 121, 139
dataism, 5
data mining, 8, 13, 95, 102, 103, 118, 153
data proxies, 10
Data Science Institute, 5
dataveillance, 84, 94, 96, 97, 139, 152
Datta, Ayona, 3, 6, 31
Day Zero, 1, 72, 77
de Goede, Marieke, 11, 84, 100
delivery, 9, 12, 18, 40, 118, 125, 135, 136, 138, 143, 152, 154
development, 2, 6, 13, 15, 17, 18, 21, 29–33, 35, 37, 42–44, 46, 47, 51–53, 65, 70, 74, 77, 86, 96, 122, 129, 142, 150, 151, 153, 159
digital activism, 18
Digital Gateway to Africa, 9
digital urbanism, 3
discrimination, 10, 11, 22, 35, 46, 48, 85, 90
displacement, 12, 22, 117
dispossession, 12, 18, 118, 120, 153
drones, 63, 66–68, 70, 76, 78, 80, 125

E

Easterling, Keller, 3, 79
ecosystem, 9, 29, 38, 41, 46, 49, 51, 142, 155
Emergency Policing and Incident Command (EPIC), 10, 83
epistemology(ies), 7, 8, 64, 149
ERP, 21, 59, 63, 70, 73, 83, 86
eviction(s), 14, 124, 156
experiment(s), 8, 59, 60, 63, 64, 66, 67, 72, 76, 77, 133
extraction, 3, 7, 12, 20, 93, 94, 118, 121, 127, 133, 134, 139, 140, 143, 150, 152, 153, 157

F

Facebook, 35, 44, 65, 90, 120, 133, 138, 159
facial recognition, 11, 62
feedback loop, 11
Ferguson, James, 16, 48
Fields, Desiree, 8, 51, 126, 142
food delivery, 12, 125, 132, 134, 136, 137, 143
Fumagalli, Andrea, 120

G

Gabrys, Jennifer, 3, 19, 79, 84, 110
gender, 10, 22, 35, 89
gentrification, 12, 16, 50, 118, 124, 127, 140, 142, 153
Geographical Information Systems (GIS), 11
Global North, 3, 121
Global South, 8, 13
Goldman, Michael, 8, 51, 142
Google, 5, 15, 65, 97, 109, 120, 132, 133, 135, 139, 157, 159
Google Sidewalk Labs, 5
governmentality, 8, 13, 16, 22, 64, 65, 85, 87, 97

INDEX   169

Graham, Stephen, 11, 85, 157, 158

H
Halpern, Orit, 7, 8, 63, 64, 133, 138,
   139, 149, 150
hawkers, 44, 53, 68
hub(s), 12, 17, 21, 30, 39–42, 50,
   51, 123, 124, 126
Hudson Yards, 5

I
IBM, 4, 15, 17, 28, 30, 47, 87, 119,
   122
India, 5, 6, 15, 29, 30, 66, 124, 129,
   134, 136, 137
inequality, 6, 9, 11, 13, 14, 16, 18,
   27, 28, 37, 39, 48, 51, 85
Infosys, 15, 125
innovation, 6

K
Kitchin, Rob, 3, 6, 7, 94, 106, 107
Konza, 5

L
land grabbing, 12, 118, 127, 142,
   153
Left Front, 15, 29
Lyon, David, 7, 84, 94–96

M
Marres, Noortje, 65, 74, 92
Masdar, 2
Mattern, Shannon, 6, 80, 85, 87, 102
Mbembe, Achille, 16
McNeill, Donald, 6, 85, 87
Mejias, Ulises A., 120
Mezzadra, Sandro, 120, 143

Microsoft, 5, 38
middle-class, 35, 45, 53, 92, 124, 130
MIT, 5
modelling, 4, 12, 22, 81, 83, 84,
   98–100, 104, 106–108, 118,
   119, 135, 141, 153, 155
models, 2, 4, 6, 9, 11, 13, 22, 62,
   72, 75, 77, 88, 89, 91, 98, 99,
   101–104, 106, 108–110, 118,
   133, 135, 138, 141, 143, 151,
   152, 157, 158
modernity, 13, 44, 120
Modi, Narendra, 5, 15, 27, 31–33
Morozov, Evgeny, 85, 140
Murakami Wood, David, 7, 84, 95

N
narrative(s), 4, 15, 16, 32–34, 40, 46,
   48–50, 92, 102, 122, 129, 131
nationalism, 15
National University of Singapore, 5
Neilson, Brett, 120
neoliberal(ism), 6, 15–17, 30, 31, 37,
   41, 42, 48, 52, 75, 129, 157
New Town Kolkata Development
   Authority, 1, 15, 30, 66
New York, 4

O
oligoptic, 7, 95
O'Neill, Cathy, 10, 11, 80, 90, 120
Ong, Ahiwa, 15
ontologies, 3, 7, 22, 158, 160

P
pandemic, 2, 66
performative, 10, 19, 34, 75, 105,
   109, 123, 138, 152
platforms(s), 2, 6, 9, 12, 17, 20–22,
   64, 84, 85, 87, 90, 92, 97–100,

170 INDEX

102, 104, 106–108, 118, 120, 125, 127, 131–134, 137–143, 151–153, 156, 158
platform urbanism, 10, 151, 153
Pollio, Andrea, 3, 16, 38, 47, 48, 51, 129, 130
post-apartheid, 37, 50, 52
postcolonial, 3, 13, 14, 31
postcolonial capitalism, 14
preemption, 7, 11, 22, 100, 106–108, 133, 152
primitive accumulation, 14
privacy, 3, 119, 158, 160
private equity, 8, 12, 117
public-private partnerships, 6, 10, 39
PWC, 17, 38, 39

R
racism, 10, 16, 108, 110, 155
Rajarhat, 12, 29, 41, 94, 117, 121, 142
RAND Institute, 4
Ratti, Carlo, 5
real-time, 2, 12, 61, 62, 66, 68, 71, 72, 74, 77, 83, 86, 88, 89, 98, 106, 107, 132
riders, 13, 136
risk alerts, 10, 89, 98, 142, 152, 155
Robinson, Jennyfer, 3, 38
Rossi, Ugo, vii, 49, 139, 145
Roy, Ananya, 15, 16, 30, 44

S
Sanyal, Kanyal, 14
SAP, 5, 20, 21, 59, 70, 71, 73, 83, 86, 87, 98, 100, 106, 122
segregation, 13, 16, 18, 37, 90, 124, 129
Senseable City Lab, 5
Silicon Cape, 9, 17, 29, 41, 46, 49, 50, 52

Silicon Valley, 9, 17, 39, 42, 45, 46, 50, 123
Simone, Abdoumalique, 14
slums, 9, 14, 30, 126
Smart Cape Access, 17, 38
Smart Cities Challenge, 17
Smart Cities Mission, 6, 15, 27, 30, 41
Smart City Strategy, 6, 17, 38, 41, 70
smart meters, 2, 61, 72, 96
smartness, 7, 28
social justice, 6, 7, 16, 23, 33, 41, 52, 78, 150
Social Justice Coalition, 18, 90
social media, 10, 18, 22, 33, 83, 90–93, 96, 97, 108, 141, 155, 159
Songdo, 2, 5, 8, 133, 139, 149
South Africa, 38
spatial justice, 2
Special Economic Zones (SEZ), 15, 142
speculative urbanism, 8, 21, 22, 29, 51, 52, 63, 84, 118, 142, 150
Srnicek, Nick, 118, 125, 127, 128
startup(s), 2, 6, 36, 47, 49, 124, 126, 142, 155
startup urbanism, 47
stock market, 12
subaltern(ity), 14
surveillance, 3, 7, 21, 44, 62, 63, 67, 68, 74, 76, 78, 84, 94–96, 118, 124, 133, 139, 140, 152, 155, 159
sustainability
sustainable, 2, 5, 35, 64, 125

T
Tata, 15, 30, 117, 130
technocracy, 3, 6
technopolitical
technopolitics, 7, 31, 37, 154

tech startups
  startup, 11, 17, 29, 36, 38, 46, 47, 125
testbed
  testbed urbanism, 8, 62–64, 139
testbeds, 2, 8, 19, 21, 63–65, 79, 150, 153
Townsend, Anthony, 4
township(s), 1, 9, 14, 15, 18, 21, 29–34, 42, 45, 48, 49, 52, 124, 126
transport, 12, 60, 61, 125, 128
trial, 71, 74
Trinamool Congress, 27, 42, 43

U
Uber, 12, 20, 22, 65, 118, 125, 127–129, 131, 132, 134, 136, 139, 142, 143, 152, 153, 156
United Nations, 5
University of British Columbia, 5
Urban Analytics Lab, 5
urban data, 9, 12, 76, 85, 87, 97, 101, 143
urban digitalisation, 2, 5, 20, 118
urban planning, 5, 6, 8, 151, 153
Urban Predictive Analytics Lab, 5
urban rights, 2
urban science, 5
urban statecraft, 21, 32, 40, 52
utopia, 4

V
value, 3, 8, 12, 20, 22, 44, 49, 68, 71, 73, 93, 118, 123, 125, 132, 134, 135, 137–140, 142, 143, 150, 152–154, 159
Vanolo, Alberto, 6, 75
venture capital, 2, 8, 12, 17, 21, 38, 46, 123, 142

W
water crisis, 1, 63, 72, 75, 77
Wesgro, 17, 38, 39
West Bengal, 15, 27, 29, 30, 33, 42, 52, 122
Western Cape, 17, 37, 39, 46
Wi-Fi, 1, 2, 39
Woodstock, 12, 39, 40, 49, 52, 124, 126, 142
world-class city, 8
worlding, 13, 15

X
Xpresso, 83–85, 90–93, 98–100, 104–106, 108, 110

Z
Zomato, 22, 125, 134–138, 142, 143, 153
Zuboff, Shoshana, 139, 140, 153